FIT AS A FIDDLE

The Musician's Guide to Playing Healthy

William J. Dawson

MENC The National Association for
MUSIC EDUCATION
1907 - 2007

Published in partnership with
MENC: The National Association for Music Education
Frances S. Ponick, Executive Editor

Rowman & Littlefield Education
Lanham • New York • Toronto • Plymouth, UK

Published in partnership with
MENC: The National Association for Music Education

Published in the United States of America
by Rowman & Littlefield Education
A Division of Rowman & Littlefield Publishers, Inc.
A wholly owned subsidary of The Rowman & Littlefield Publishing Group, Inc.
4501 Forbes Boulevard, Suite 200, Lanham, Maryland 20706
www.rowmaneducation.com

Estover Road, Plymouth PL6 7PY, United Kingdom

British Library Cataloguing in Publication Information Available

Library of Congress Cataloging-in-Publication Data

Dawson, William, J.
  Fit as a fiddle : the musician's guide to playing healthy / William J. Dawson.
    p. cm.
  Includes index.
  ISBN-13: 978-1-57886-683-0 (hardback : alk. paper)
  ISBN-10: 1-57886-683-9 (hardback : alk. paper)
  ISBN-13: 978-1-57886-684-7 (pbk. : alk. paper)
  ISBN-10: 1-57886-684-7 (pbk. : alk. paper)
  1. Music—Performance—Health aspects. 2. Instrumentalists—Health and hygiene.
  3. Overuse injuries—Prevention. I. Title.
  ML3820.D38 2008
  781.4'3—dc22   2007025726

⊗™ The paper used in this publication meets the minimum requirements of
American National Standard for Information Sciences—Permanence of
Paper for Printed Library Materials, ANSI/NISO Z39.48-1992.
Manufactured in the United States of America.

CONTENTS

FOREWORD

There has always existed a considerable lack of insight into how performers react to and deal with the many problems that musicians often acquire in practice sessions and performance venues. Up until now there has not existed one readily available source that clearly and succinctly deals with these concerns. Dr. William Dawson's wonderful new book, *Fit as a Fiddle*, is a perfect companion for all performing musicians who wish to understand and concern themselves with good musical-performance health.

Musicians seldom possess training and background in medicine. As teachers and performers, we tend to answer the problems that accompany our hours of practice and performance with "home remedies" rather than with any real medical knowledge and understanding. Musicians and music teachers usually teach according to handed-down traditions established by their teachers who likewise have not had serious medical training. Similarly, there are few individuals trained in medicine who have a knowledge or interest in musical performance and who possess the kind of musical ability and talent that might instruct musicians.

William Dawson, MD, is a performing musician who has specialized for many years in addressing the physical problems that often afflict performing musicians. He is one of the very few who has, as a trained musician and a medical doctor, effectively been able to bridge the gap between the two worlds of music and medicine.

Seldom, if ever before, have the physical concerns of the performing musician been addressed so clearly and so knowledgeably. *Fit as a Fiddle* is an exceptionally well-written and easily understood guide to identifying and addressing virtually every problem associated with musical performance. Dr. Dawson's book will become a valued and indispensable resource for every performing musician and teacher of music.

Frederick L. Hemke, DMA
Louis and Elsie Snydacker Eckstein Professor of Music
Charles Deering McCormick Professor of Teaching Excellence
The School of Music
Northwestern University, Evanston, Illinois

ACKNOWLEDGMENTS

Writing any medically related book cannot be done in a vacuum, even though the subject matter reflects the writer's many decades of personal, medical, and musical experience. A great number of people have played significant roles in helping me bring this project to fruition. To each and every one, both named and unnamed, I give my thanks and appreciation.

I am particularly indebted to the International Double Reed Society, publisher of *The Double Reed* and *The Journal of the International Double Reed Society*, and to Dr. Ronald Klimko, its bassoon editor, for the permission to revise, expand, and reprint information presented in several articles previously published in those journals.

Also, I wish to express my appreciation to my many hundreds of musician patients and musical-research subjects for their willingness to share with me the finer points of their special physical needs as instrumentalists and for providing many technical and artistic details about their instruments. I appreciate their tolerating my many questions about their specific musical activities, and I know that I have learned even more from them musically than they may have gained from me medically.

Two members of my family deserve special thanks. My daughter, Susan Dawson-O'Brien, professor of journalism at Rose State College, provided not only critical and thoughtful editing of the manuscript but also a great deal of photographic assistance in preparation of the illustrations. My wife, Beverly, has endured my absences during the many years spent in medical practice and making music, as well as the additional time spent researching these subjects and transforming a vast amount of data into words; to her goes my unending gratitude for her patience, understanding, support, and love.

William J. Dawson, MD

INTRODUCTION

WHY I WROTE THIS BOOK

Instrumental musicians—as well as vocal musicians, dancers, and actors—can and do experience physical problems that may interfere with their practice and performance. They need knowledgeable, caring help to recognize, treat, and prevent such problems. For more than thirty years I was fortunate to be able to combine my interests and love of both medicine and music into an orthopedic and hand surgical practice that focused on the problems of instrumental musicians. In addition, as a performing instrumentalist and private teacher, I have talked with countless musicians about a wide variety of physical difficulties that have interfered with their music; most of these involved their hands and upper extremities. During these years, many music teachers, physicians, and therapists have questioned me about their own students or patients, seeking advice and guidance to help their students or improve their diagnostic and treatment skills.

Until recently, it was difficult for many performers to get answers to their medical questions. Relatively few physicians and therapists specialize in the twenty-five-year-old field of performing arts medicine, and many are not yet aware that this specialty even exists. Furthermore, others also treat musicians, dancers, and actors, but only as a part of their usual practice.

Some health-care professionals are or have been musicians or dancers themselves and thus can bring to their practice some of the knowledge and awareness of the special needs of musicians and other performing artists. Sadly, many other practitioners have traditionally taken another, more simplistic, route to the treatment of performance-affecting problems, essentially saying to the patient, "If it hurts when you do it, then don't do it." This same advice was unfortunately prevalent in the treatment of athletic injuries and many other conditions as little as thirty years ago. However, advances in medical knowledge and skill, coupled with the determination of athletes to avoid such a black-and-white approach to diagnosis and treatment of their problems, have resulted in the high quality of sports medicine care available today throughout the country.

I wrote this book to further the current expanding interest in improving the availability, quantity, and quality of health care for all performers. It began more than a decade ago as a series of articles I had written for the *Journal of the International Double Reed Society* and *The Double Reed* quarterly periodicals. Because of the recent expansion of knowledge in performing arts medicine and the many performers and educators who might benefit from it, I have made major additions to these articles and also inserted several new chapters focusing on additional current and useful topics.

The information in this book is intended to answer many questions asked by instrumental musicians and their teachers about some general health problems that may affect musical performance, with an emphasis on those that involve the hand and the entire upper extremity (including the shoulder). Large national studies have shown that approximately two-thirds of musicians' physical difficulties involve the musculoskeletal system, and the upper extremity is by far the most common anatomic area involved in this population.

WHO CAN BENEFIT FROM THIS BOOK?

The intended readership for this book is extensive. Currently there are more than 160,000 professional instrumentalists in the United States alone, both performers and teachers, plus approximately 20,000 students enrolled in American collegiate and conservatory music programs. In addition, a recent Gallup poll, reported in the *International Musician*, estimated that sixty-two million amateur instrumentalists are actively playing in the United States today; this impressive figure includes more than one hundred thousand members of community bands and many thousands more who are enrolled in the academic music programs of our primary and secondary schools.

Any instrumentalist, whether or not he or she currently has a problem with hands or upper extremities that affects musical performance, may benefit from the information contained in this book. Music teachers at all levels also will find useful details in these chapters, knowledge that may be applied to help recognize and deal with their students' physical problems or, it is hoped, prevent such problems altogether. To all those readers who wish to learn more about medical problems affecting performers, with a special emphasis on rehabilitation following treatment or prevention of repeated problems: please read on!

Each of the articles I previously published was originally written to stand alone, and the entire series was written over several years. Because of this, the reader may notice some duplication of information and references from one chapter to another. I have chosen to retain many of these duplications strictly for the purposes of emphasis and convenience. A number of the points presented in these chapters are crucial to the basic message of this book, and they deserve to be repeated. I ask each reader to bear with me on this important matter.

A WORD ABOUT THE SUGGESTIONS FOR FURTHER READING

This book is not a textbook of performing arts medicine; excellent ones currently exist. Nor is it an exhaustive or encyclopedic listing of all the medical problems that can affect performers and all the possible treatments for them. Some readers will wish to delve more deeply into the subjects discussed not only in the following chapters but also those that go beyond this book. For them, I have concluded each chapter with Suggestions for Further Reading, a selection of references pertinent to the chapter's specific topic. Several textbooks on performing arts medicine and some of its specific components are included among the references; by and large, they contain a broad range of information on many pertinent topics and can serve as a single general source for many interested readers. The bibliographies contained in many of these books and articles include a number of additional useful references for the reader who seeks further information.

The vast majority of publications containing these articles can be found in most medical or musical libraries. In addition, a relatively comprehensive bibliography of articles, books, and other sources is available on the website of the Performing Arts Medicine Association at http://www.artsmed.org.

SUGGESTIONS FOR FURTHER READING

Brockman, R., P. Chamagne, and R. Tubiana. 1991. The upper extremity in musicians. In *The Hand,* vol. 4, ed. R. Tubiana, 873–86. Philadelphia: W. B. Saunders.

Middlestadt, S. E., and M. Fishbein. 1989. The prevalence of severe mus-
    culoskeletal problems among male and female symphony orchestra
    string players. *Medical Problems of Performing Artists, 4,* 41–48.
Sataloff, R. T., A. G. Brandfonbrener, and R. J. Lederman, eds. 1998.
    Textbook of Performing Arts Medicine, 2nd ed. San Diego: Singular
    Publishing Group.

PLAYING WITH PAIN

MAKING MUSIC IS PHYSICAL

Playing a musical instrument involves an incredibly complex series of physical actions. It is extremely difficult to attempt separat-
ing the act of musical performance into its specific mechanical and
physiologic components; they are multiple in number, overlapping
in scope, and frequently different from one instrument to another.
Nonetheless, if we were to try, a partial list logically might begin by
describing the myriad anatomic positions and muscular forces
needed to hold or support a musical instrument.

Second, the rapid, complicated, and often endlessly repetitive
motions required to play various musical passages are dependent
upon the nature of the instrument and its sound-producing mechanism and are performed primarily by the upper extremities (although most percussionists and organists might take exception
with this statement). Wind instrumentalists, in contrast to string or
keyboard performers, must incorporate an additional variety of
specialized oral and respiratory manipulations, since sounds from
these instruments are produced by the movement of an air column

generated by the musician's own breathing apparatus and controlled in great part by the embouchure.

Body movement is an integral part of this process—making music is not a static activity. From the comparatively compact finger motions needed to depress the keys of a clarinet to the global motions of hands and arms while beating out a jazz solo on a drum set or bowing a stringed instrument, musical performance is physical. The musician must be aware not only of those postures and movements involved in picking up and supporting an instrument, or sitting or standing in front of it, but also of the multitude of specific and precise motions needed to move the various keys, valves, slides, sticks, pedals, and other devices to change the pitch of the sound or to produce percussive sounds. Different musical instruments require different ranges of joint motion to play; in addition, no two people play an instrument in precisely the same physical way. Furthermore, various types of music may require the performer to play a given instrument with different techniques to produce the specific sounds required by the composer.

Playing as many as forty musical notes per second places great demands on the hands and fingers. It requires, among other things, integrity of the many small and large bones in these areas, plus intact and flexible ligaments that hold the bones together and help form the joints. The bones must line up so the fingers point in the correct directions, while the joints must move far enough, and in the right alignment, to accomplish all the motions needed for these complicated acts. The tendons must glide smoothly to move the bones into the positions required for playing.

Every tissue or structure in the hand has a complex nerve supply for both sensory input and motor (muscle) control; I'll go into nerve anatomy and basic functions in the following chapter. In the palm of the hand, all these anatomic structures are covered by a tough, specially modified type of skin that permits repeated pressure and abrasion without damage to itself or to the underlying components. An injury can affect any or all of these structures and the way they function.

PROBLEMS CAN DEVELOP

Almost all of us have experienced headaches, stiff necks, and sore backs from time to time. Minor pains such as these are usually temporary and do not interfere significantly with life's activities; we learn to deal with them as a routine part of living. However, at times painful conditions become severe enough to interfere with making music.

Pain often results from problems and conditions that affect the musician's hands and upper extremities. These conditions can have a profound and deleterious effect on making music, whether performing in concert or playing for one's own enjoyment. The disabilities produced by these problems affect the quality and quantity of musical performance and often can pose a serious threat to an individual's life in music (professional or avocational).

For convenience, I will classify these problems into two basic categories: occupational and nonoccupational. Those conditions that arise directly from playing music are, of course, considered occupational, while all others are classed as nonoccupational. Both types may have an effect on the playing of one's instrument. The multitude of nonoccupational hand problems are not as well recognized and not as widely discussed as those related directly to music making; nonetheless, the effect of both categories of problems on instrumental performance and career may be equally devastating.

A MUSCULOSKELETAL EMPHASIS

Each topic in this book has significance for, and application to, most instrumentalists. This includes both playing-related disorders and those nonoccupational difficulties that also can interfere with practice and performance. Although the primary emphasis is on problems affecting the hands and wrists, I discuss a number of other general and musculoskeletal problems that may affect the entire person; the interrelationships among these topics are usually quite obvious and definitely can be useful to the reader.

Why should we concentrate on the bones and joints? Large surveys of symphony and opera musicians (undertaken by Dr. Hunter Fry from Australia and by Drs. S. E. Middlestadt and M. Fishbein from the University of Illinois) have shown that approximately two-thirds to three-quarters of high-level instrumentalists have developed one or more music-related musculoskeletal difficulties during their performing lifetime. These problems affect the musician's hands and wrists more frequently than any other parts of the body. Recognizing and minimizing the potential effect of such problems on a performer's career requires awareness and knowledge of the problem so that it can be identified and dealt with in the most effective manner.

TYPES OF PAINFUL PROBLEMS

Pain in any part of the musculoskeletal system can arise from many causes. We can place those that are pertinent to the instrumental musician into six basic categories: overuse conditions, inflammations, nerve entrapments, injury, arthritis, and various miscellaneous reasons. Succeeding chapters cover each of these six categories at greater length, but an introductory overview should help to put them into perspective.

Over the past twenty years, many authors have used the term *overuse syndrome* extensively in journals and other publications devoted to performing arts medicine and other musical topics. The pain resulting from overuse may originate in muscles, tendons, ligaments, or fascia. It is produced by physical stress on these structures to a degree greater than they can tolerate, and most often it is due to a combination of excessive time and intensity of musical playing or practicing. Other frequent causes are improper playing techniques and other associated activities.

According to medical researchers, overuse-related problems occur most frequently among string players and pianists, with wind, brass, and percussion performers affected much less commonly. They can occur in musicians of all ages and levels of skill, from the young amateur to the performing professional. In general, continued playing only tends to make these symptoms worse.

Tendinitis and its companion condition, *tenosynovitis*, are commonly used terms for various pains in the wrist or elbow and sometimes as improper but generic terms for any upper extremity pain. However, these inflammatory conditions only affect tendons and their coverings and are located only in the specific body areas where tendons are present. Overuse activities can sometimes cause tendinitis, but they are not the only cause.

A less frequent cause of pain is *compression of nerves*. The performer may describe a feeling of numbness or tingling in one or both hands and also may experience muscle weakness or problems with coordination (clumsiness). Nerves may be compressed or pinched at any point from the neck down to the palm of the hand; this can produce such problems as *carpal tunnel syndrome*. Occasionally nerve compression can be caused by a specific musical activity, but more often it is due to other causes.

Injuries can produce some of the most acute, troublesome, and painful conditions a performer can experience. Because of this, they rival the overuse syndrome as the primary source of a musician's concern about the ability to perform. Rarely do musical performances or related activities cause injury directly; much more frequently the trauma is due to sports or other nonmusical pursuits. My clinical data on medical problems affecting nearly fourteen hundred instrumentalists over a fifteen-year period reveals that injury or trauma was the principal cause of difficulties affecting their hands and upper extremities. Within this large group, nearly half were injured by playing sports.

Many musicians may develop *arthritis*, a group of painful conditions characterized by inflammation of the body's joints. The most common type of hand arthritis is *osteoarthritis*, also known as degenerative joint disease or "wear and tear" arthritis. It frequently involves the small joints of the fingers nearest the fingernails but can affect the thumbs and wrists nearly as often. In some instances osteoarthritis may result from injury to a joint, but more commonly it occurs in people of middle age and older years who do not have a history of joint trauma.

A second type of arthritis is called *rheumatoid arthritis (RA)*. It is much less common than osteoarthritis but can be more devastating to functions of the hands and wrists; it usually begins at a younger age and often progresses much more rapidly than osteoarthritis. The knuckles and middle joints of the fingers are affected very frequently, but the wrists, elbows, and shoulders may be involved also. In addition, the spine and lower extremities also may be involved. Like osteoarthritis, RA produces joint swelling, stiffness, and pain; however, RA usually results in greater loss of joint motion, less stability in the affected joints, and more interference with one's everyday activities.

COMMON SYMPTOMS AND SIGNS

Pain is one of the most common symptoms experienced by instrumentalists and can be produced by all of the conditions I've mentioned above. People can describe its severity in many ways, but perhaps the most useful characterization is according to the degree to which the pain interferes with one's musical and other activities.

Swelling of the hands or arms is another sign. It most often is associated with injury or trauma, especially around joints, but it also can occur as a result of arthritis or other inflammations. Of all the upper extremity joints that may become swollen, the middle knuckle of a finger usually is the most significant and deserves our closest attention. Trauma to this joint is perhaps the most common cause of swelling; the patient frequently minimizes the difficulties, but very often such an injury can become a source of permanent disability.

Deformity (the presence of abnormal shape or alignment of a body part) also may be an important sign of injury. Unless both right and left sides of the performer's body have been injured, a "normal" side is usually available to both patient and physician for visual and functional comparison. The appearance of an obvious deformity is a most compelling reason to urgently seek professional medical help. When deformity is caused by injury or trauma, acute pain usually is present as well.

SUFFERING IN SILENCE

Until quite recently the "injured" musician usually was forced to suffer in silence. Admitting any illness or physical disability was viewed as a threat to one's employability, since every performer was expected to play at 100 percent capacity at all times, and a long list of skilled, healthy musicians waited to fill an empty chair. Furthermore, no musician wanted others to know that he or she was seeing a physician.

In past years, only a few physicians knew much about the special problems of musicians and were sympathetic to their needs, and little information existed in the medical literature to help them care for such a specialized population. The common advice, "If it hurts when you play, then stop playing," obviously was not proper for a professional instrumentalist, and most of those who received it promptly sought other opinions, hopefully more favorable to their cause. However, in the past twenty years these philosophies have changed drastically and positively, as the field of performing arts medicine has developed and expanded worldwide into a full-fledged occupational medical specialty.

The Performing Arts Medicine Association has become the primary professional organization devoted to this new specialty. The member physicians, therapists, and other health professionals who have dedicated themselves to caring for musicians, dancers, and actors now can offer them sympathetic awareness and precise knowledge of their special requirements and difficulties. These arts medicine professionals also possess the scientific and technical skills required for the diagnosis, treatment, rehabilitation, and prevention of many of the problems affecting performers.

In addition to arts medicine specialists, numerous primary care and specialty physicians, many of whom also are trained musicians or dancers, have become skilled and experienced in this unique discipline and provide a significant contribution to the care of all performing artists. Injury, whether or not caused by making music, now has become a respectable topic for discussion and action by musicians of all degrees of skill and involvement, and its artistic and economic significance has gained increasing recognition by labor unions and by administrators of many performing organizations worldwide.

WHO TREATS THE MUSICIAN?

As I mentioned above, many instrumentalists (as well as singers, dancers, actors, and other performers) often were reluctant to seek formal medical care for their problems. Instead, they often turned to practitioners of alternative therapies and health philosophies for relief of their pain and other difficulties; they perceived these practitioners as being more attuned and sympathetic to their special conditions and needs. Some of these healers would include osteopathic, chiropractic, and naturopathic physicians; podiatrists; physical and occupational therapists; other therapists who specialize in massage, dietary manipulations, and reflexology; and practitioners of body awareness techniques such as the Alexander and Feldenkrais techniques. These health professionals continue to play a major role in treatment and prevention of many performers' problems and frequently work in close harmony with the more traditional medical physicians in treatment of complex problems.

Most musicians who need to visit a "traditional" medical doctor (MD) have a wide range of physicians from which to choose. They can obtain care from one of several types of primary physicians, such as a family doctor or general practitioner, a specialized family practitioner, an internist or general medical specialist, and even from some knowledgeable pediatricians and adolescent medicine physicians. In addition, a large spectrum of specialists often participate as consultants; this group includes orthopedic and hand surgeons, rheumatologists, neurologists, physiatrists or rehabilitation specialists, and, on occasion, psychiatrists.

The number of health professionals who practice some form of performing arts medicine continues to grow. Full-service performing arts medicine clinics currently are operating in more than twenty cities in the United States alone.

WHAT CAN BE DONE?

Specific treatment of any painful problem or injury best begins with an accurate diagnosis. Next is the initiation of precise care: methods include rest, practice modifications, medication to reduce inflammation or pain, corrective exercises, splinting, or physical changes in playing. The health professional's choice of treatment method(s) must be based on the patient's specific problem and his or her musical requirements. For example, a physician or an occupational therapist may devise hand or finger splints to be worn by some musicians during practice sessions and performances. In this way they may be able to maintain a reasonable level of musical activity during the healing process.

Pain is a warning signal that often is produced by our bodies when incorrect or abnormal body use or various physical problems occur. Experience has shown that it is wise to heed the symptom, not ignore it. The doctrine of "no pain, no gain" has proven over the years to be detrimental in dealing with most physical problems, including those of athletes, dancers, and musicians. The health professional can help interpret and treat this symptom and its causes most effectively, as well as provide valuable assistance in restoring correct use of the involved area without producing additional damage in the process.

Various adaptations in musical techniques can aid in promoting effective and comfortable playing without causing further physical damage. Healing of injured or overused parts may be facilitated by using techniques such as splinting for their protection during painful periods. Instrument modifications, such as an elevated shoulder pad or chin rest for the violinist or an adjustable right thumb post for the oboe, can decrease physical stress from unnatural playing postures. Many instruments can be fitted with a neck strap or floor post, so the performer does not have to support instrument weight with the hands, arms, shoulders, or back.

One extremely important factor in treatment is obtaining support and assistance of the instrumental teacher (when appropriate) in defining and eliminating the musical causes of pain. A knowledgeable teacher can be of great help by devising corrective musical exercises to aid the performer's return to comfortable and effective playing. In addition, using various relaxation and body awareness techniques, such as Alexander or Feldenkrais, may relieve muscle tension and thus improve playing comfort and endurance.

NOTE

Portions of this chapter were adapted from an article by Dr. William Dawson that appeared in *The Double Reed*, Winter 1988; © The International Double Reed Society, Idaho Falls, ID. Reprinted by permission.

SUGGESTIONS FOR FURTHER READING

Cantwell, J. 1987. The legend of Cantwell da Jeanci. *The Double Reed,* *10(2)*, 54–56.

Dawson, W. J. 1986. Reed maker's elbow. *Medical Problems of Performing Artists, 1*, 24.

Dawson, W. J. 1997. Common problems of wind instrumentalists. *Medical Problems of Performing Artists, 12(4)*, 107–11.

Fry, H. J. H. 1986. Incidence of overuse syndrome in the symphony orchestra. *Medical Problems of Performing Artists, 1*, 51–55.

Fry, H. J. H. 1986. Overuse syndrome of the upper limb in musicians. *Medical Journal of Australia, 144*, 182–85.

Hochberg, F. H., R. D. Leffert, M. D. Heller, and L. Merriman. 1983. Hand difficulties among musicians. *Journal of the American Medical Association, 249*, 1,869–72.

Levy, C. E., W. A. Lee, A. G. Brandfonbrener, J. Press, and A. E. Levy. 1992. Electromyographic analysis of muscular activity in the upper extremity generated by supporting a violin with and without a shoulder rest. *Medical Problems of Performing Artists, 7*, 103–109.

Middlestadt, S. E., and M. Fishbein. 1989. The prevalence of severe musculoskeletal problems among male and female symphony orchestra string players. *Medical Problems of Performing Artists, 4*, 41–48.

Williams, G. 1987. Taking pains: Musicians who learn to relax. *The Double Reed, 10(3)*, 62–63.

2

SOME BASICS OF STRUCTURE AND FUNCTION

Although courses in human anatomy and physiology are not a usual part of instrumentalists' musical education, these musicians have learned many elements of bodily structure and function through earlier education and life experiences. Knowing how our bodies are put together and how they work is essential to understanding the physical activities involved in making music and the problems that may arise from these activities. In this chapter I clarify some of the definitions and concepts of anatomy and physiology and present them in logical (but not simplistic) fashion, using lay terms instead of potentially confusing medical jargon.

FRAMEWORK—THE BONES AND JOINTS

Bones are the body's framework; in healthy people they are solid and unyielding to all stresses except severe force and trauma. They form the main support for all other body structures, by encasing them (as in the skull and chest) or acting as a place for their attachment (muscles and ligaments). Most bones in the extremities

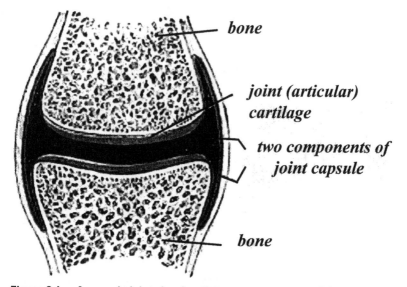

bone

joint (articular) cartilage

two components of joint capsule

bone

Figure 2.1. A generic joint showing the two components of the joint capsule (outer fibrous and inner synovial layers), as well as the joint space and articular cartilage

have a long, tubular shape but vary considerably in length. Their ends are modified to form *joints*, spaces between adjacent bones where movement may occur. The ends of these bones are covered with a thick cap of *cartilage*, a smooth, shiny, resilient substance that permits effortless gliding of one surface on another.

Each movable joint in the extremities is surrounded and supported by structures called *ligaments* and *joint capsules*. Ligaments are strong fibrous bands or sheets that attach to the bones near their cartilage surfaces and serve to hold the bones together. The joint capsule is a multilayered fibrous sac that surrounds the bone ends and (usually) the ligaments, making the joint watertight. This arrangement is necessary because a thick fluid produced by the innermost layer of the capsule lubricates the cartilage surfaces, and the fluid must not leak out of the joint.

All movable joints possess a certain degree of stability, a condition that permits motions in only certain ranges and extents. The direction and extent of movement at each joint is governed by the shape of the bone ends and by the shape and placement of the ligaments. Some joints, like the shoulder, are constructed with looser ligaments and large-capacity joint capsules and thus can move widely in many directions. On the other hand, these flexible joints have less stability and greater mobility than, for example, a finger joint.

The ability of a joint to move in various directions is related to its configuration or shape. The upper extremity, that part of the body extending from shoulder to fingertips, contains a variety of configurations, including ball-and-socket joints (shoulder), hinge joints (finger), and saddle-shaped joints (at the base of the thumb). Two bones form each of these articulations, yet each has different possible motions. When additional bones are added to the configuration, as in the case of the elbow or wrist, rotation and hinge-type motions also become possible. The number and arrangement of the ligaments becomes more complex to facilitate these additional movements.

MOVEMENTS—THE MUSCLES AND TENDONS

Musical function depends on movement: lining up the various body segments into their appropriate positions, then moving them in the ways necessary to produce musical tones. The muscles produce these motions. Simply stated, virtually all muscles originate and terminate on the bones, and their contraction produces movement at the joints.

Muscles are composed of the following four basic functional parts.

1. The fleshy portion or *muscle belly* is able to contract and relax, thus changing its length and diameter; this is accomplished by a series of complicated chemical reactions. We can observe the

Figure 2.2. Left forearm muscles, front (palm) side

effect by contracting the biceps muscle in the front of our arm, just above the elbow. The belly or contractile segment varies in size and shape from one muscle to another, but each is "designed" to move a specific joint in a specific range with a specific degree of force or power.

2. Often the muscle must move a joint that lies some distance from its contractile segment. To do this, the force of contraction is transmitted through strong fibrous "ropes" called *tendons*. These are attached at one end to the muscle belly and at the other to a bone on the opposite side of the joint to be moved. Tendons may be flat or cordlike, and they vary in length from fractions of an inch to as much as ten inches. When tendons must move over a hand or finger joint, or glide smoothly in a tight area, thin tubes of tissue containing synovial fluid, the same lubricant found inside joints, surround them. This cushions and protects the tendon from rubbing and kinking during its to-and-fro movements.

3. Both the muscle belly and its tendon (if present) are generally attached to bones. A very short, firm tendon structure anchors the fleshy part, while the end of the tendon contains special fibers that insert directly into the bone.

4. Surrounding and within most muscles are thin sheets of fibrous tissue known as *fascia*. These firm, unyielding layers separate the different sections of some muscles and also separate one muscle from another. This arrangement makes it possible for one contracting muscle to glide smoothly over another.

Muscles are arranged singly or in groups, depending on the specific joint movements they produce. Some groups of muscles move a joint in one direction, while other groups move it in the opposite direction. If both opposing groups contract simultaneously, the joint does not move but is said to be *stabilized*. This action holds one part of the body immobile while another, more distant joint

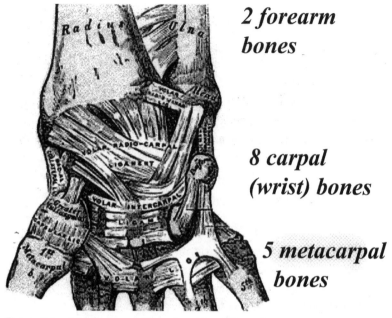

2 forearm bones

8 carpal (wrist) bones

5 metacarpal bones

Figure 2.3.   Ligaments on the palm side of the wrist

moves to allow performance of a specific task. A typical example of near-joint stabilization to permit more distant joint movement is a flutist's right shoulder. The flutist's shoulder stabilizes to allow movement of the fingers. The opposite action of distant stabilization for near-joint motions can be seen in the right (bow) hand of string players. The bow hand holds the bow firmly while the wrist, elbow, and shoulder move to draw the bow across the strings.

A muscle or group of muscles that performs a single movement is known as an *agonist*, while its opposing muscle or group is called an *antagonist*. When both agonists and antagonists contract simultaneously, little if any joint movement occurs. If joint stabilization is not the desired goal of this action, then both groups would seem to be working at cross purposes. These inefficient *co-contractions* ultimately may cause fatigue of the involved muscles by maintaining a state of continuous contraction without allowing them to rest.

Muscle rest is needed to permit the release of lactic acid and other chemical byproducts of the contraction process. Fatigue results in a loss of endurance, when the muscle cannot perform repetitive and strong contractions over a prolonged period of time.

CONTROL APPARATUS—THE NERVES

Muscle contractions begin with an electrochemical stimulus that is applied to specialized areas within the muscle belly. This stimulus travels through a number of nerve fibers that begin in the spinal cord and extend outward to supply the muscle.

Nerves are a part of our body's "electrical system" and generally originate in the brain and spinal cord. They travel throughout the body, bundled together like cables composed of many fine "wires" or filaments. These so-called *peripheral nerves* transmit impulses from the brain to all the muscles (*motor functions*) and from many tiny structures in the skin and other tissues back to the brain and spinal cord (*sensory functions*). Elements of sensation such as pain, touch, pressure, heat and cold, and position awareness begin in various microscopic sensory "organs" located throughout the body. They are especially numerous in critical areas such as the hands and face. The brain recognizes and makes sense of the input it receives from all these sensory nerves. On occasion the body is called upon to react quickly to some of these sensations, especially if they're dangerous or unpleasant. In such cases, the brain sends lightning-like impulses outward through the motor nerves to the appropriate muscles, causing them to contract and thus move that part of the body away from the troublesome or potentially harmful stimulus.

Some of these nerves supply our arms and hands. Several large nerve bundles leave the neck, on both sides of the vertebrae, and travel behind the collarbones into the areas under the arms. Here they separate and trace their individual paths down the inside, front, and back of the arms to the wrists, sending out many branches as they go. The most distant branches, those that supply the hands and fingers, contain many tens of thousands of individual nerve fibers. The greatest concentration of nerve endings in the entire upper extremity is located in the fingertips; this explains why these areas are so sensitive to touch, pain, and differences in temperature. These tiny but important "threads" are in part responsible for all the very precise and critical sensations that we perceive in our hands and fingertips, as well as for the complex and coordinated motions needed to accomplish the multitude of different tasks that makes up everyday living.

Although some nerve fibers have sensory functions and some motor, the two groups work together very efficiently. As I mentioned before, a painful sensory perception produces a rapid response in the motor nerves supplying the painful area, moving the body parts away from the painful stimulus. Similarly, an instrumentalist must be aware of body position (a sensory function) to move hand or fingers just the right amount (motor function) to finger or bow the next note in a musical passage or to adjust the embouchure for tone production or proper intonation. Correcting intonation by minuscule changes in finger or embouchure position is the result of a feedback process that begins with the hearing nerve acting as the source of sensory input and ends with the contraction or relaxation of the appropriate muscles to make the desired adjustment. This process is repeated over and over again, often many times per second, until the correct result is achieved and heard.

The upper extremity contains three large nerves that supply most of its muscles and sensory nerve endings. All three are critical for proper instrumental performance. Each one supplies sensory input from a separate area, with very little overlap.

The *radial nerve* winds around the back of the upper arm to the outer side of the elbow. It then proceeds down the outer side of the forearm to the back of the hand, supplying sensation to the skin of this area and motor function to the muscles that extend the elbow, wrist, thumb, and major finger knuckles.

The *median nerve* courses down the inner front side of the arm, the front of the forearm, across the front of the wrist, and into the palm of the hand. It supplies sensation to the front of the forearm and wrist and to the palm side of the thumb, index finger, and long fingers. The muscles it supplies produce flexion of the wrist, fingers, and thumb.

The *ulnar nerve* lies behind the median nerve in the arm. It travels behind the inner elbow bone (the "funny bone") and comes to lie on the inner side of the forearm and front of the wrist. It supplies sensation to these areas and to the palm side of the ring and little fingers. The muscles innervated by the ulnar nerve control most of the fine, precise functions of the thumb and fingers.

SUGGESTIONS FOR FURTHER READING

Gray, H. 1974. *Gray's Anatomy: The Unabridged Running Press Edition of the American Classic.* Eds. R. Howden and T. Pick. Philadelphia: Running Press.

LeVay, D. 1988. *Human Anatomy and Physiology,* 3rd ed. Chicago: NTC Publishing Group.

3

TEACHER AND STUDENT

A musician's playing life can last many decades. Consider the fact that students can start the Suzuki string program as early as age three or four and that some beginning piano students are not much older. Most elementary school music programs in the United States begin in the fourth grade, long before a child's body has completely matured and before adult bodily proportions and capabilities have been attained. Now, let's fast-forward through many decades of making music, in varying degrees of intensity and frequency, to consider the many adults who still perform regularly while in their late eighties. Although the advantages of favorable genetics cannot be denied, other factors also are at work, allowing these seniors the opportunity to play with continuing skill and in relative comfort despite the normal physical effects of aging. One of the most important factors is beginning early with good practice and performance habits.

The phrase "starting a student off right" is meaningful in several ways. Certainly the nature and quality of early musical training is crucial in developing proper instrumental or vocal technical skills. Beyond this, however, are the many factors involved in healthy playing, so necessary to permit a lifetime of making music and enjoying the activity. When pain or disability enters the picture, it may adversely affect one's love of music and the ability to spend a large part of one's life making it. Prevention of playing-related disorders is the ultimate goal of all those who are involved in performing arts medicine, and there is no better time to introduce a student to this concept than in the first months and years of musical activity.

Physical problems *can* and *do* occur in young musicians and for a variety of reasons. Several published studies have documented the incidence of overuse difficulties in students, even those as young as seven or eight years of age—long before they might have any clue or insight into the cause of their problem or what to do about it. As one might expect, the vast majority of these overuse difficulties were playing related. In addition, acute injuries in childhood are exceedingly common, and many of them also can affect the ability to play an instrument; in my experience of treating hundreds of musicians younger than twenty-one years of age, acute injury or trauma was the cause of more than 75 percent of their hand and upper extremity problems.

PLAYING-RELATED PROBLEMS

The music teacher can and should play a pivotal role in helping students develop healthy playing practices. All music teachers must be aware of their students' potential for developing medical difficulties and have a layperson's working knowledge of their causes, contributing factors, basic diagnostic elements, and principles of (nonmedical) treatment and rehabilitation. Whether in the private studio or working in groups, whether the student is a beginner or in an advanced conservatory program, instruction in the basic principles of healthy playing can greatly benefit a young person's musical life and provide a solid foundation for later self-awareness and care of medical problems related to practicing and performing. Teachers can provide this help in two different but related ways.

The first way is helping to prevent playing-related physical problems, primarily those that are related to musical overuse or misuse. Beginning instrumentalists need precise and usually repeated instruction in correct posture and use of body mechanics for holding and playing any instrument, whether while sitting or standing. They need to learn just how much muscle activity (strength and speed) is needed, and from which muscles, to produce the right sounds. The clear corollary to this concept is learning how to avoid using more muscles than necessary to do the job properly.

In an ideal world, music teachers would be familiar with the basic anatomy and physiology of music making, but this is often not the case. Nonetheless, most teachers can explain and demonstrate the elements of correct playing technique quite well in lay terms, based on their own education and playing experience. This explanation ideally should include cogent reasons for their beliefs and descriptions of the long-term benefits for the student when he or she follows such advice. These basic principles should be incorporated into each lesson, especially for beginning students on any instrument. As the students become more skilled, the teacher should observe them regularly for compliance in these techniques and offer appropriate reminders when proper techniques are lacking. In my experience, use of excessive muscle tension and improper postural changes are the two most common technical reasons for a teacher to take this type of corrective action. For brass players, teachers should be watchful for excessive mouthpiece pressure and caution against too much practicing, which can lead to overuse problems.

Physical mismatches between the musician and the instrument can also cause difficulties, and music teachers must make sure their students have a properly sized instrument. For example, orchestra directors should understand the difficulty that can be caused by playing a viola that is too large for the performer's arms and hands, and band directors should start out young bassoonists on a bassoon made for smaller hands. Marching bands pose additional problems, and directors need to be familiar with problems that develop from shouldering and marching with instruments, such as a tuba that is too large and heavy for a young musician's small frame.

A second component of teacher involvement is developing the awareness and ability for early recognition of physical problems that can adversely affect a student's playing abilities. Many of these problems are painful, and a troubled student generally shows some outward evidence of this pain while playing or shortly thereafter. I encourage all teachers to observe their students closely as they play, not just listen to the music they produce. A new abnormal physical action, such as grimacing while playing, or assuming a different posture of torso, head, neck, or arms, may be a warning signal that something is not right. Other evidence of developing problems might include a shaking of one hand after putting the instrument down or stretching the neck or shoulders during a rest period. Generalized fidgeting is another frequent sign of physical discomfort, even though the student may not be aware that he or she is actually doing it.

Once the instructor becomes aware of any overt or subtle negative expressions and actions, the student should stop playing, and the teacher should try to investigate the new "symptom." One doesn't have to be medically trained to have this type of awareness and concern nor to ask some appropriate, commonsense questions of the student.

When the student and teacher can agree that a problem exists, the next step is trying to determine whether there is a relationship with any of the elements of making music. In many cases, the teacher may recognize that some element of technique or practice has changed more rapidly than the student's capability to adapt, and this change has resulted in the painful condition. Such changes may include increased practicing without taking appropriate breaks, working too intensely, or repeating a passage excessively without getting it right—these are but a few of the myriad causes and contributing factors in playing-related pain.

Other causes may be relatively obscure, such as the nearsighted child developing neck or shoulder pain caused by straining to see the music. Some students can recognize and verbalize their problem and possibly be aware of causal relationships, while others need their teacher's help to recognize and understand the circumstances.

The logical conclusion to this whole process is, of course, making modifications in playing practices that are appropriate to the perceived cause of the painful or mechanically incorrect condition. Simple reminders of proper posture or embouchure, greater relaxation of "uninvolved" body areas, taking a five-minute break from practice every twenty-five or thirty minutes, or similar changes may be enough to solve the problem entirely. Other students may benefit by trying a different way of supporting their instrument (this is especially true with woodwind and upper string players) or a modification of bowing technique. It is not only appropriate but also mandatory for the teacher to consider and implement all these forms of "treatment"; most health professionals have not learned the intricacies of musical technique or the special physical requirements for playing each instrument.

For the instructor who begins teaching an advanced student, the process perhaps can be even more difficult. The student may have developed and used troublesome habits and patterns, both physical and musical, for a long time, possibly for many years. These are more difficult to identify, understand, and solve. Always make any changes in these students' playing slowly and gently, and expect the resulting progress to be gradual, not dramatic. Making changes too rapidly or intensely could lead to the development of additional difficulties, often while not really solving the original one. It also is best not to modify multiple elements of a student's musical technique all at once; this would be like trying to change a golfer's swing by altering several components during a single lesson!

TRAUMA AND INJURY

Many conditions can affect musical performance; in the child and adolescent, most of them are not related to making music. Childhood accidents seem to be endemic and have many different causes; perhaps the most common is participation in sports. Falls are the second most common cause and also can produce potentially severe damage to all parts of the body. For most instrumental musicians, acute injury to the hand and the rest of the upper extremity would seem to be the most devastating and certainly would be more likely to interfere with playing than, for example, a broken foot.

For many students (and all other musicians as well), the time that must be spent away from one's instrument because of trauma depends on many factors. It is possible, even with some hand or wrist injuries, to allow a limited or modified return to playing at the same time active treatment is still under way. How easily and rapidly this is done depends on the nature of the injury, the student's willingness to try playing, and getting knowledgeable guidance from an understanding physician or therapist about activities they should attempt or avoid. I always encourage frequent and open communication among the student, parents, music teacher, and health professionals to ensure that optimum medical care can continue, while at the same time ensuring that the return to music is not unduly delayed.

The music instructor may be able to provide part of the rehabilitation for some injuries, especially those involving the upper extremity. Musical exercises may be devised to facilitate joint movements and to improve muscle strength and coordination—and such exercises do the trick perhaps more effectively than some traditional medical-therapy routines.

NOTE

Portions of this chapter were adapted from an article by Dr. William Dawson that appeared in *The Double Reed*, Summer 2001; © The International Double Reed Society, Idaho Falls, ID. Reprinted by permission.

SUGGESTIONS FOR FURTHER READING

Brandfonbrener, A. G. 2000. Epidemiology and risk factors. In *Medical Problems of the Instrumentalist Musician*, eds. R. Tubiana and P. Amadio, pp. 171–94. London: Martin Dunitz.

Dawson,W. J. 2006. Playing without pain—strategies for the developing instrumentalist. *Music Educators Journal, 93(2)*, 36–41.

Manchester, R. A., and S. Park. 1986. A case-control study of performance-related hand problems in music students. *Medical Problems of Performing Artists, 11*, 20–23.

Shoup, D. 1995. Survey of performance-related problems among high school and junior high school musicians. *Medical Problems of Performing Artists 1995, 10*, 100–105.

OVERUSE

Many physical conditions can affect the ability to make music. Among the most common of these are problems directly related to playing an instrument. Consider these facts:

1. A musician's hands and arms (and, for some, their embouchure) must perform hundreds of individual motions and actions every second in order to play the required notes.
2. Most performers play many hours each week.
3. A musical life or career may last for more than seventy years.

It is no wonder, then, that the body is likely to develop various problems related to musical overuse. The upper extremities are affected most frequently by these conditions, although the neck and other portions of the spine also may be involved. Overuse-related difficulties are extremely common among high-level instrumentalists at one time or another during their performing careers. However, overuse-related problems also affect many non-musicians, especially in the areas of sports and certain nonmusical occupations. This topic has gained much attention in newspapers, magazines, and other media in the past decades, especially as overuse relates to occupations that use computers and keypunch equipment.

Overuse is known by many names and is defined differently by various authorities. Synonyms include *cumulative trauma disorder, overuse syndrome, repetitive strain injury, occupational strain syndrome, repetitive motion disorder, occupational cervicobrachial disorder, tendinitis,* and *regional pain syndrome,* among others. All these terms imply that the affected person has experienced a greater degree of physical stress, force, or repetitive activity than his or her body can tolerate and that certain symptomatic conditions have resulted from this experience. Confusion about these terms is compounded by several medical authors who include nerve compression problems and other neurological conditions within the spectrum of overuse. Currently there is no single classification or definition of overuse that is recognized by the majority of medical practitioners. This problem has been studied and discussed by members of the Performing Arts Medicine Association and by other occupational groups.

WHAT IT IS

I've chosen a comparatively simple definition, designed to make sense to performers, educators, and health professionals alike. Overuse can be considered as *a practice or activity that may produce one or more musculoskeletal symptoms and can negatively affect the function of a specific anatomic area.* It is characterized by excessive physical use (force, duration, or repetition) of that area while performing a specific activity, musical or otherwise. The degree of excess varies from person to person; so can the location, severity, and duration of symptoms that may result from overuse.

It is important to differentiate overuse from two closely related terms, *misuse* and *abuse.* Overuse implies that the involved area of the body is being used correctly but to an abnormal degree and that no physical or structural changes are produced in the overused tissues. By contrast, misuse usually is caused by an incorrect activity, such as using poor or improper physical techniques or mechanics to perform any task, or by a "mismatch" between the individual and the instrument (for instance, a small-framed person trying to play a full-sized viola). Abuse describes an improper or damaging use of the body that usually occurs in a willful, conscious manner. To compound the confusion, two or more of these "-use" problems may occur simultaneously and may be related to the same cause or type of action. Excessive overuse or misuse, especially if the musician feels the specific activity is necessary, actually may lead to abuse and to the physical changes that usually accompany it.

WHAT HAPPENS IN OVERUSE

When body tissues are injured by overuse activities, they react in certain specific and predictable ways. For example, muscles that must contract frequently or forcibly for a prolonged period have a chance neither to rest and replenish the chemicals needed for further contraction nor to get rid of the lactic acid and other waste products of their metabolism. Further muscle use under these conditions produces pain and decreased performance; movements are slower and less forceful, and there is less endurance for continuous use. This situation is as true for instrumentalists as it is for runners, tennis players, and anyone who may use his or her muscles excessively.

The basic physical changes or reactions in all overused tissues are a result of the repetitive activity to which these structures are exposed; in more severe cases, this activity produces a variety of microscopic changes, including abrasion, tearing, or stretching of muscle tissues, tendons, ligaments, and other supporting structures around the joints. All these tissues then can become swollen and irritated, resulting in inflammation or some type of "-itis" (tendinitis, arthritis, bursitis, synovitis, etc.). Persistent overuse usually results in these changes and symptoms becoming chronic. The ultimate effects of chronic overuse, if not properly treated, may include permanent thickening or tightening of the overused structures, resulting in a loss of motion, flexibility, strength, or endurance in the involved area.

CAUSES

A variety of activities, musical and otherwise, may be described as overuse practices. In many cases they can produce medical conditions, which are accompanied by physical symptoms. I have found it helpful to consider this relationship in regard to three factors described by the performing arts specialist Dr. Hunter Fry:

1. Abnormal playing techniques
2. Increases in the product of (time) x (intensity) of musical activity
3. Relationship to various genetic conditions

The first of these factors often relates to abnormal or unusual postures, movements, or forces during playing. For instance, a fatigued person may slump or collapse his torso, and his back may become rounded. In compensation, the neck must extend and lift the head up to see the music stand and the conductor. Another common technical mistake is playing with excess physical force on the keys, valves, slides, or strings or using sticks and mallets with unnecessary tension; this, too, can often produce unwanted physical symptoms. Other similar causes exist as well, some of which may be obvious to the player (or to an observer) and others that are much more subtle but equally disastrous.

A related and extremely common cause of overuse is a rapid or sudden change in practice patterns, often as a result of one or more changes in a person's musical life. These changes might include a new school, teacher, job, or instrument, beginning or emphasizing an additional or different instrument, or undertaking new and more demanding repertoire. Many performers and students must adapt to these changing circumstances without sufficient professional guidance or specific instruction, and often the changes are abrupt. It takes a certain amount of time and personal practice to properly and comfortably achieve new motions, forces, and patterns of musical technique; without a gradual training and conditioning process, physical difficulties are likely to ensue.

An additional cause of symptoms for some is the addition of, or change to, a new nonmusical occupation, especially one that requires new or unfamiliar physical activities. The physical requirements of many jobs, which most people may consider to be normal or benign, actually may create conditions or difficulties that can interfere with the normal mechanics of musical performance.

Playing patterns change for every person with the passage of time and in response to different life activities; it is these changes, among others, that can affect the "time x intensity" factor I mentioned above. Young instrumentalists are most likely to experience overuse when they enter a new school or conservatory, return to school in the autumn after a musically inactive summer vacation, or increase the amount and intensity of practice in preparation for recitals, juries, or auditions. In many of the above circumstances there is an abrupt change in practice time and intensity, and the body cannot adapt successfully to this rapid alteration.

The basic spectrum of overuse-related problems that can be produced under these circumstances is similar to that seen in the athlete who begins a new sport, or returns to an old one, without proper training or reconditioning. Certainly a new job, musical or otherwise, also may require significant changes in one's physical activity and can, at times, result in one or more of these overuse conditions or syndromes.

Genetic factors in overuse are not as easy to describe, and neither the physician nor the musician can alter them. In some cases the size of an individual's hand or arm may not be suited to the playing of a specific instrument. This discrepancy may explain why overuse-related problems are seen in women more than in men and in violists more than violinists. The female hand is generally smaller that that of the male and has a proportionately lesser degree of muscle strength; when these facts are combined with the larger size of the viola, the reason for this increased prevalence of playing-related difficulties becomes clear. Similarly, young instrumentalists may develop problems if their instrument is too large to play comfortably. Some performing arts medicine authorities classify this type of problem under the heading of misuse, not overuse; they believe it is caused by an apparent mismatch of personal equipment (body size and structure) with the size of the instrument or its component parts.

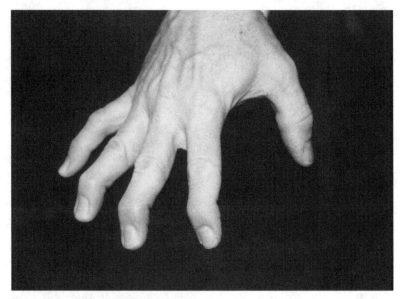

Figure 4.1.   Hypermobility of fingers

Dealing with these size discrepancies has resulted in modified instruments, such as unusually shaped violas and smaller or more closely spaced keys on some student wind instrument models. The need to avoid or modify such mismatches also helps explain the popularity of smaller-sized instruments, such as the violins, violas, and cellos advocated by the Suzuki method.

An additional genetic factor is the variability of individual persons' connective tissues and their ability to tolerate excessive physical stresses. Some people are more likely to experience problems from overuse than others, even though the degree of stress may be the same for each. A congenital physical condition that seems to be associated with the potential for increased overuse-related difficulties is *hypermobility,* or what many people describe as "being double-jointed." People with this condition, which is present normally in 5 to 8 percent of the population, have comparatively loose ligaments around the joints; this laxity allows the joints to move more widely than those of normal people (figures 4.1 and 4.2).

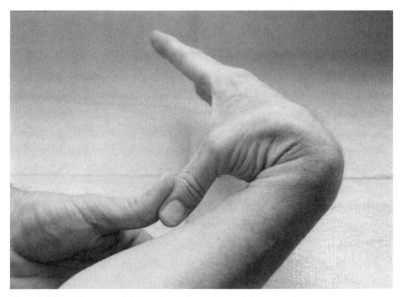

Figure 4.2.   Hypermobility of wrist and thumb ligaments

Hypermobility can result in unstable joints, especially in the hands and fingers, and is seen frequently in instrumentalists. The outer finger joints may "collapse" or hyperextend as they press down upon the keys or strings; to compensate for this, the performer must use the finger flexor muscles more vigorously and in different patterns. If this compensation is not performed in a careful and organized way, the abnormal patterns of use may lead to muscle strains.

SIGNS AND SYMPTOMS

Instrumentalists may experience a variety of symptoms from overuse activities, depending on what body tissues are affected and the degree to which they are involved. The most common symptom is *pain*, which usually occurs at the point of maximum damage. It may occur only with a particular musical activity and may or may not continue after the activity has ceased. For some people it may occur with nonmusical activities as well but may have been aggravated by playing one's instrument. In still other instances this pain may be severe enough to interfere with all hand activities and may cause the player to temporarily discontinue all use of the affected hand(s) or arm(s).

Musicians also may experience other symptoms with some frequency, including swelling or thickening, warmth, feelings of stiffness or tightness in joints or muscles, a sense of decreased flexibility or coordination, "locking" or "catching" of a finger or thumb, and muscle tiredness or fatigue following repetitive physical activity.

Certain parts of the body are more likely to develop overuse difficulties than others. The small *intrinsic muscles*, which lie between the hand bones (*metacarpals*) and at the base of both the thumb and little finger, can become strained and painful with abnormal or overly stressful repetitive finger or hand use. Indeed, small muscles are more likely to develop such problems than large ones like the biceps (upper arm) or trapezius (neck) because they have less capacity to restore themselves after heavy use. Tendons can become roughened and inflamed as they glide through their tight passageways on both sides of the wrist and at the base of the fingers.

Muscle pain after overuse activities occurs more frequently on the back (*extensor*) surface of the forearm and also at the outer elbow bone (where the extensor muscles originate). The larger muscles of the shoulder, neck, and back may feel strained or tight after excessive use and then go into a protective, painful contraction that may restrict movements of these areas; this type of contraction is described medically as *spasm*.

A number of musical instruments can produce specific patterns of overuse-related problems. The pianist's right hand and fingers, for example, are more likely to be involved than the left, perhaps because the right hand needs greater activity to play the majority of melodic lines. In contrast, violinists and violists are more likely to experience problems with their left, or fingerboard, hand; this phenomenon is related primarily to the awkward positions they must assume both to hold the instrument and to depress the strings. Playing larger stringed instruments, such as the cello and double bass, may produce painful overuse-related symptoms in the musician's shoulders or upper back because these musicians constantly need to hold up the arms for both bowing and fingerboard use.

Wind instrumentalists are not immune to overuse either, although their problems are less prevalent than those of keyboard and string players. Supporting the weight of an instrument on the performer's hands may cause pain and ultimately may lead to a lack of stability in various joints; this situation is most noticeable in the right thumb of oboists, English hornists, and clarinetists (figure 4.3), as well as in the left hand and palm of flutists and bassoonists. The cramped playing position of the fingers on the oboist's right hand also has been implicated as a cause of pain and strain.

When the health professional examines a musician with an overuse-related problem, he or she may notice several common findings.

Figure 4.3. Note the clarinet's weight resting entirely on the performer's right thumb.

The affected area often is painful to touch or probe and also may hurt when it is used or moved by the patient. Muscles involved in the overuse process may hurt when they contract, as well as when they are stretched out passively by either the patient or the examiner. Swelling often is painful, especially if it is located within a joint or caused by a collection of fluid around inflamed tendons in the hand. Uncommonly, the patient may notice some decreased sensation in the fingers often accompanied by a feeling of numbness or tingling; this condition is produced when nerves are compressed as a result of some forms of overuse.

TREATMENT TECHNIQUES

This section outlines only the basic and commonly accepted philosophies and methods of treatment that may be prescribed by the physician or other health professional; I make no attempt here, or anywhere in this book, to recommend or detail specific treatments for specific problems. Each musician should seek skilled and appropriate evaluation and care for any music-related condition by consulting a health-care professional in his or her community who is familiar with such problems. Since most performing arts medicine practitioners are located in major cities or larger urban areas, musicians who live in other areas may need to explain in much greater detail to their own practitioners about their special physical needs, playing requirements, specific symptoms, and other concerns.

Regardless of what type of medical practitioner the musician sees, several factors can help make the first visits most useful to both parties. When calling to make the initial appointment, the musician must tell the office staff that he or she is an instrumentalist and preferably tell them the instrument played. Second, if it is possible to bring one's instrument to the office visit, I heartily recommend that the musician do this. Even though the examining physician may not have any knowledge about playing a specific instrument, seeing it being held and played may be of tremendous help in determining what is wrong with the patient. This is especially true if the musician's problem occurs only while playing. I know of several physicians who have an electronic keyboard in their offices for just such purposes, and I have gladly welcomed tubas, contrabassoons, and cellos into my office over the years.

The principal method of treatment is to avoid or modify the overuse activity that caused it. In most cases a period of *rest* is part of the initial care. Unless the problem is extreme, absolute rest is rarely used nowadays, since totally avoiding all use of the affected area usually produces unwanted weakness and a loss of general (and musical) conditioning. Instead, a period of relative rest, involving avoiding or modifying those painful activities, seems to be equally effective and has the advantages of minimizing weakness and loss of both dexterity and technique.

Many musicians have experienced occasions when they must decrease both the time and intensity of musical practice sessions because of pain in various areas of their upper extremities, neck, or back. Local treatment, such as the prescribed use of protective splints or braces, can assist in providing rest for some of these areas. Using these appliances not only can limit unwanted motions and forces about various joints but also can encourage the affected tissues to heal more rapidly and completely.

Pain also may respond to a variety of medications. In many cases a period of rest alone is effective in decreasing the performer's pain, but in some circumstances additional pain-relief (*analgesic*) medication may be indicated. The choice, dosage, route, and duration of these drugs should be medically prescribed and should be appropriate for the specific patient and his or her problem. Some types of pain medication can be purchased over the counter, but in many cases a prescription is necessary.

One of the most important methods of overuse treatment is musical, not medical. Some change of practice and performance habits and techniques is mandatory in treating most forms of musical overuse conditions. For many, this may begin by relearning how to hold and play the instrument in a physically relaxed and physiologically efficient posture, avoiding the muscle tension and cramped hand positions that so often are a cause of pain. For many instrumentalists, their music teacher or coach can be of great help by recognizing that the player indeed has a problem caused by musical overuse and by devising appropriate changes in repertoire, practice emphasis, and techniques to minimize or alleviate that problem.

Since the instrument itself so often is the cause of overuse difficulties, modifying it in various ways may also help significantly to relieve symptoms and prevent recurring or future problems. This form of treatment is especially important for many performers who, for a variety of reasons, are unable to limit their playing time or intensity to the extent needed for proper relief of symptoms. In many cases these alterations can be made quite simply and do not require the expertise of a trained technician, nor do they require the musician to part with the instrument for a prolonged period.

The tilted-head playing posture of many violinists and violists has been implicated in the production of chronic neck and shoulder strain. Adding a shoulder pad or rest to the underside of the instrument can effectively alter this stressful position by lifting it into a more comfortable position (figure 4.4). Additionally, using a modified chin rest may decrease stress on the neck and shoulder muscles by lessening the sideways head tilt and the left rotation of the chin. These rests come in a variety of sizes, are usually available in most areas, and are not too costly.

Some simple techniques can decrease excessive pressure on wind instrumentalists' hands and fingers. Using a neck strap for the clarinet (figure 4.5), oboe, or English horn minimizes the strain on the performer's right thumb caused by the instrument's weight. It works effectively whether one plays sitting or standing. A floor peg can support longer instruments, such as alto or bass clarinets or English horn, and is very effective in decreasing the force and stress on the player's right thumb. A flutist can obtain special padded rests or supports for the right thumb and the surface of the instrument where it rests upon the left palm. These rests distribute the instrument's weight over a larger area of skin and protect both the skin and the underlying nerves from excessive pressure.

Modified thumb rests are available for oboists and clarinetists as well and can be found in many woodwind or double reed specialty shops. Some provide a greater space between the instrument barrel and the performer's thumb, which allows the fingers of the right hand to contact the keys at a more comfortable angle. Other rests provide support to all weight-bearing areas of the thumb and adjust to multiple hand sizes and support postures. All these are small and lightweight, can be attached and removed quite easily, and cause no damage or permanent alteration to the instrument.

One doesn't have to depend on a teacher for advice on practice modifications; each instrumentalist should feel empowered to take

Figure 4.4. A shoulder rest allows the violinist's head to remain upright and helps to avoid raising the left shoulder.

Figure 4.5.   Using a neck strap decreases the clarinet's weight on the right thumb.

the initiative and make some of these changes personally. Doing this successfully depends on using one's common sense; recognizing the problem and making these changes early in the course of overuse-related pain may limit the extent and length of symptoms. Based on many years of both personal and professional experience, I have found four specific techniques that can greatly decrease the stress of any practice session and are also useful in preventing problems in the healthy musician. I recommend to all teachers that they use them with their students. The techniques are:

1. Play or practice only twenty-five minutes out of every thirty; get away from the instrument and do something else for the other five. Do this for practice sessions of any length, and especially if the session is vigorous or intense. The break also helps the musician's mind by temporarily leaving a source of

mental stress and allowing a more effective refocus when re-turning to the practice session.

2. Use the same principles of warm-up as practiced by athletes. Spend a few minutes stretching your muscles and joints to gain increased flexibility (see the exercises in chapter 10); tightening and contracting help warm up the muscles used both at the instrument (playing posture) and to actually play musical notes.

3. Vary the musical stress in each practice session. Don't con-centrate on a single piece or passage for long intervals; doing this repetitively can be a form of overuse.

4. If you become aware of bodily discomfort or pain during a practice session, stop playing *immediately*. Try to determine the nature and cause of the problem. Resume playing only af-ter you are pain-free, relaxed, and reasonably aware of how to prevent a recurrence of the pain.

SUGGESTIONS FOR FURTHER READING

Charness, M. E. 1992. Unique upper extremity disorders of musicians. In *Occupational Disorders of the Upper Extremities*, eds. L. H. Millender, D. S. Louis, and B. P. Simmonds, pp. 227–52. New York: Churchill Liv-ingstone.

Dawson, W. J. 2000. Upper extremity overuse in instrumentalists. *Medical Problems of Performing Artists 15(2)*, 66–71.

Dawson,W. J. 2002. Upper extremity problems caused by playing specific instruments. *Medical Problems of Performing Artists 17(3)*, 135–40.

Dawson, W. J., M. E. Charness, D. J. Goode, et al. 1998. What's in a name—Terminologic issues in performing arts medicine. *Medical Problems of Performing Artists 13(2)*, 45–50.

Fry, H. J. H. 1987. Prevalence of overuse (injury) syndrome in Australian music schools. *British Journal of Industrial Medicine 44*, 35–40.

Fry, H. J. H. 1989. Overuse syndromes in instrumental musicians. *Seminars in Neurology 9*, 136–45.

Fry, H. J. H. 1991. The treatment of overuse syndrome in musicians: Results in 175 patients. *Journal of the Royal Society of Medicine 81*, 572–75.

Lippmann, H. I. 1991. A fresh look at the overuse syndrome in musical performers: Is "overuse" overused? *Medical Problems of Performing Artists 6(2)*, 57–60.

TENDINITIS AND TENOSYNOVITIS

Many people, medically trained or not, feel that these two conditions belong with the group of overuse-related difficulties as a more convenient way to describe or discuss them. Others have used *tendinitis* as a catchall term to describe any painful condition involving one's hands, wrists, forearms, or elbows. Most medical authorities, however, believe that tendinitis and tenosynovitis are distinct entities; I do as well, and I think they deserve a chapter of their own in this book.

Two major facts serve to separate these conditions from the often nebulous or general diagnostic terms used to describe many overuse-related problems. First, tendinitis and tenosynovitis are related to a specific pathological process, *inflammation*, unlike the muscle strains and diffuse regional pain syndromes I described in chapter 1. Second, overuse activities often are not the only causes of tendinitis or tenosynovitis; these conditions frequently arise as a result of specific diseases and other causes.

DEFINITIONS

Tendinitis can be simply defined as an inflammatory condition of a tendon. It may occur where the tendon originates or where it inserts into bone; a common example is the so-called *tennis elbow*, which occurs at the outer bony prominence of the elbow. A second common location is in the central part of the muscle unit, where the tendon is attached to the fleshy muscle belly. Tendinitis also may begin within the substance of the tendon, between its attachments. This latter type of inflammation, regardless of its location, may be associated with preexisting degenerative changes occurring within the tendon, usually as a result of aging or microscopic repetitive trauma.

Tenosynovitis is defined as an inflammation of the gliding (*synovial*) coverings of a tendon and often is accompanied by similar changes on or within the tendon itself. It can develop wherever tendons glide back and forth within their coverings or sheaths. In most cases this occurs in restricted areas of the body, including both the back and front of the wrist where the tendons are held closely to the underlying bones during movement. Another common location is at the thumb side of the wrist; inflammation within this tendon "compartment" is called *De Quervain's tenosynovitis*.

In the hand itself, the tendons that flex the fingers into a fist move through tight fibrous tunnels adjacent to the hand and finger bones. These tunnels are lined with gliding tissue also, but repetitive, forceful activity can produce inflammation that frequently results in some thickening of the tendon. The thickened tendon often "catches" on the entrance to the tunnel in the palm during motions, producing a type of tenosynovitis commonly known as *trigger finger*.

CAUSES

The most common cause of both tendinitis and tenosynovitis is repetitive motion or force within the muscle-tendon unit. Making music is not the only cause of these motions and forces; indeed, many different occupational and leisure activities have been implicated in this process. Forceful activities generally tend to produce problems at the bony origin or insertion of the tendon, as I described above in relation to tennis elbow. Repetitive motions without excessive force are more likely to cause inflammation about the tendon sheaths or gliding structures. Both overuse and misuse practices or activities, whether musical or otherwise, may produce tendinitis in various locations. For example, an instrumentalist may experience pain at the elbow from repeatedly grasping or holding an instrument with excessive force, or a percussionist may experience tendinitis on the back of the wrist as a result of repetitive motion and excessive forcefulness.

Tenosynovitis is also well recognized as a complication of certain diseases. Perhaps the most common of these is *rheumatoid arthritis (RA)*, a generalized inflammatory disease that affects the gliding surfaces and coverings of tendons in more than one-third of the people afflicted with it. The tendons and other tissues become degenerated as a result of the inflammation, resulting in thickening or fraying. In some patients, especially those who are untreated or in whom conventional therapies have failed, these tendons may become so frayed and eroded that they rupture—a complication that limits active movements of the fingers or wrist and represents a serious threat to an instrumentalist's career.

SYMPTOMS AND SIGNS

Pain is the most common symptom of tendinitis; it usually is confined to the irritable or inflamed area of the tendon or to its junction with the muscle belly. Pain may be produced or aggravated by actively contracting the muscle, especially against external resistance, or by passively stretching the muscle. In more severe cases, the muscle or tendon may be painful even when the limb is at rest.

Other physical signs may be present, either singly or in combination. The tendon and its gliding coverings may become thickened or swollen; one can see or feel the changes easily in tendons that lie just under the skin. *Crepitus*, a crackling or bubbling sensation, may be felt under the skin when an examining finger touches over the tendon or the patient moves it actively. The tendon or its bony origin or insertion also may hurt when it is touched. In cases of trigger finger, movement of the involved digit may be limited by pain or inability of the thickened tendon to glide through its sheath, and the patient often cannot extend it from a flexed or partial fist position. When the problem is less severe, the finger may be able to move back and forth, but a clicking sensation may accompany this movement; the clicking may or may not be painful.

TREATMENT PRINCIPLES

Simply put, effective treatment involves controlling not only the inflammation but also its underlying cause. For the active instrumentalist, achieving only one of these two results may not be sufficient to relieve the process and prevent recurrences.

Various medications can decrease the severity of inflammation and relieve some of its symptoms. Many types of medicines may be prescribed—some given in the form of pills taken by mouth and others injected directly into the inflamed area. The choice of medication, its dose, the method of administration, and the duration of use must be determined on an individual basis by the treating physician, based on the nature and severity of the problem.

Adequate treatment of the underlying inflammatory disease process, when present, is paramount. This is especially important in the case of severe conditions such as RA. Often a medical specialist such as a rheumatologist can provide the expertise needed to deal with the disease from a number of different standpoints (medication, protective splinting, various forms of therapy, lifestyle changes, etc.).

Perhaps the more difficult part of treatment, especially for the musician, is finding ways to decrease the amount of motion and force when using the muscles—this being the primary cause of music-related inflammation. As in the case of overuse-related problems, resting the affected area is important. In addition, both physical and occupational therapists may provide significant assistance by instructing the patient in specific modifications of both general and occupational activities, fabricating splints for actively inflamed structures and helping to strengthen and retrain other muscle groups that may minimize the excessive demands on inflamed tissues.

Conservative treatment may not be successful in all patients diagnosed with tendinitis or tenosynovitis. This is especially true when the condition is associated with rheumatoid arthritis, but it also is relevant in the case of trigger digits and De Quervain's tenosynovitis. If the problem has failed to respond adequately, surgical treatment should be considered. In some severe cases of tenosynovitis, removing the diseased, thickened gliding tissues permits the tendons to move freely and minimizes the danger of rupture. Trigger digits and De Quervain's problems can be released merely by enlarging the opening of the tendon tunnel. Most of these procedures can be done safely and conveniently under local or regional anesthesia in an outpatient setting, and early use of postoperative therapy can facilitate a rapid return to usual activities. Surgery in patients with generalized inflammatory diseases must be considered as just one part of the treatment, however, and not curative in and of itself.

SUGGESTIONS FOR FURTHER READING

Charness, M. E. 1992. Unique upper extremity disorders of musicians. In *Occupational Disorders of the Upper Extremities*, eds. L. H. Millender, D. S. Louis, and B. P. Simmonds, 227–52. New York: Churchill Livingstone.

Dawson, W. J. 1992. The role of surgery in treating musicians' upper extremity problems. *Medical Problems of Performing Artists* 7, 56–62.

Rozmaryn, L. M. 1993. Upper extremity disorders in performing artists. *Maryland Medical Journal* 42, 255–60.

CARPAL TUNNEL AND
OTHER NERVE PROBLEMS

The subject of pinched nerves has been the source of considerable media coverage over the past two decades. This is partly due to its relationship to job-oriented injuries and partly because the prevalence of these problems in the general population is on the rise. In particular, carpal tunnel syndrome has become a frequent topic of conversation and concern among many occupational groups as well as among individuals.

Earlier, I discussed the difference between nerves that transmit information from the peripheral parts of the body to the brain (sensory nerves) and those that supply impulses to muscles (motor nerves). Interfering with the function of each type of nerve can produce specific and different symptoms, which can be recognized by the person so affected.

Nerve compression or "pinching" can occur in instrumental musicians as well as in people engaged in many other activities; however, it is not always related directly to playing one's instrument. A great variety of activities and conditions can result in pressure on the body's nerves. In this chapter I describe and explain a number of nerve compression conditions that may be pertinent to the musician and present some information that should help the performer to recognize and care for them. Most of this information relates to nerve compression problems in the neck and upper extremities, because this is where the most frequent and functionally significant difficulties (for musicians at least) usually occur.

COMPRESSION—WHY AND WHERE?

At several locations in our bodies, nerves pass near anatomical structures that may cause pressure on them and thus produce symptoms. We're all familiar with the *tingling* felt in our ring and little fingers when we strike our "funny bone" at the inside of our elbow. However, less acute and more steady pressure on a nerve also can cause tingling and pain in the area of the body supplied by that nerve—and this area often may be located far away from the actual site of compression. Prolonged nerve pressure can lead to the feeling of *numbness* in these areas also; this is the "falling asleep" sensation we may experience in our feet if our legs are crossed for too long.

The motor nerves react to pressure in a different way. When they are compressed abnormally, the muscles they supply function less vigorously or efficiently; in these circumstances a person may become aware of *weakness* or a clumsy feeling while trying to perform a particular task that requires the action of these muscles. Chronic or long-standing pressure can lead to a loss of the nerve supply to certain muscle fibers, and in severe cases these muscle fibers waste away and the muscle becomes smaller and weaker; physicians call this condition *atrophy*.

Nerves can be compressed or pinched from both occupational and nonoccupational causes. In addition, problems with certain nerves and anatomic locations are likely to be related to specific diagnoses and conditions, and characteristic patterns of symptoms are seen with each of them.

The most common location for nerve pressure to occur in the upper extremity is at the base of the palm, where the hand joins the wrist. Two major nerves, the *median* and the *ulnar*, pass from the forearm into this region in separate, parallel canals or "tunnels" (figure 6.1). *Carpal tunnel syndrome* is that combination of symptoms produced when the median nerve is compressed in its tunnel, which is located between the two fleshy, muscular areas at the base of the palm. A patient with this condition usually experiences pain,

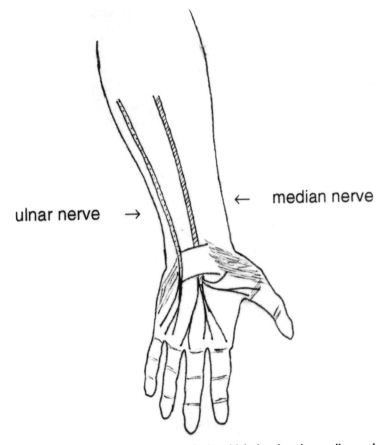

ulnar nerve →   ← median nerve

Figure 6.1.   Diagram of the wrist (palm side) showing the median and ulnar nerves

numbness, or tingling in the thumb, index finger, and long fingers; in severe or long-lasting cases, weakness of the muscles at the base of the thumb may occur and cause a person to drop objects from a loss of grip strength.

Carpal tunnel syndrome has received much recent notoriety in the press because of its occupational connection with computer users and supermarket checkers, but it can be caused by *any* activity that produces repetitive forced flexion of the wrist toward the palm. For some people, musicians included, merely holding one's wrist flexed for a few moments may precipitate these symptoms.

The ulnar nerve lies less than an inch away from the median nerve at the wrist, closer to the little-finger ("pinky") side of the hand. Here it is subject to pressure from a variety of nonoccupational situations, including riding a lightweight bicycle with underslung handlebars (this area of the hand rests squarely on the lower portion of the handlebar). Symptoms of ulnar nerve compression from this mechanism are very similar to those produced by pressure on the inside of the elbow described above; however, only the palm side of the hand and fingers gets numb, not the back.

In the neck, large nerves can be compressed by abnormal (*bulging* or *herniated*) discs (resilient fibrous "cushions" located between adjacent neck bones or vertebrae) or by small bony overgrowths (*spurs*) that develop on the edges of these bones as a result of degenerative or "wear and tear" arthritis. This type of nerve pressure may produce symptoms of pain between the patient's shoulder blades or down an arm and may be accompanied by feelings of numbness in a forearm or hand. When the motor portion of the nerves has been involved also, the patient usually complains of clumsiness or weakness when using a hand or arm.

These same nerves can be pinched in a second area of the neck, located more to the front, between the neck muscles and the uppermost rib. Compression at this point may produce a condition known as *thoracic outlet syndrome*. This syndrome often is aggravated by poor neck and shoulder postures and is seen most often in people with very sloping shoulders and poor muscle tone; it can produce many of the same symptoms that we see with disc problems in the neck, although very few people complain of true muscle weakness on the affected side.

Another common site of pressure is the inner side of the elbow, an area I mentioned previously in this chapter. The ulnar nerve lies here in a bony groove behind the lower end of the arm bone (the *humerus*) and is at risk for irritation by repetitive or constant external pressure. This nerve supplies sensation to the little finger and controls many of the small muscles in the hand. Symptoms of ulnar nerve compression often include numbness and tingling in the little finger, weakness of finger pinch, and perhaps some clumsiness during precise manual motor activities (writing, doing buttons, etc.). This constellation of symptoms is known as *cubital tunnel syndrome*.

RELATION TO OVERUSE—DOES IT EXIST?

Some authorities have included nerve compression problems with other effects of overuse practices; they reason that repetitive motions of the upper extremity, with the limb held in an abnormal posture, actually produced the nerve impingement. While this assumption may be true for certain performers, I prefer my definition of overuse and the conditions it can produce. It also seems more convenient to consider all nerve compression problems at the same time, rather than to divide the topic in an arbitrary fashion. Therefore, let's consider two compression syndromes related directly to overuse in musical performance.

The left arm of violinists and violists must be held in a distinctly abnormal position to facilitate correct placement of the fingers on the strings (figure 6.2). The degree of elbow flexion (bending)

Figure 6.2.   Violinist's left hand in first position

Figure 6.3. Violinist's left hand in eighth position

changes as the fingers move to the higher string positions (figure 6.3), thus requiring repetitive and often rapid flexion and extension (straightening) movements of the left elbow. This type of physical activity has been implicated in causing *cubital tunnel syndrome*, a condition characterized by compression and irritation of the ulnar nerve in its bony groove behind the elbow.

These repetitive motions seem to present a greater potential problem for individuals who also have hypermobility syndrome and who therefore may have an abnormally mobile ulnar nerve at this location. With increasing flexion of the elbow, the nerve tends to ride up along the edge of the groove; in some cases it actually may come out of the groove toward the front of the elbow when the joint is flexed completely. When this phenomenon occurs regularly over a prolonged period of time, it may produce chronic inflammation and scarring around the nerve. Players afflicted with this combination of difficulties usually experience numbness and tingling in their ring and little fingers during maximum or forced flexion of the left elbow, and those with severe degrees of compression may complain of clumsiness while using their left fingers on the strings, as well as difficulty in holding the instrument firmly with the left thumb.

Pianists also can develop music-related nerve compressions. Those performers who use the so-called "high wrist" position while playing (figure 6.4) may place themselves at increased risk for developing carpal tunnel syndrome. Constant use of the wrist in a highly flexed position can cause excessive pressure on the median nerve. The same type of pressure can occur in the right hand of bassoonists who hold the instrument in an abnormally rotated manner that requires excessive wrist flexion, as well as in electric bass players. I personally have not seen an electric bassist who plays with a straight right wrist, since the shape of the instrument and the position in which it is held seem to mandate a severe degree of right wrist flexion.

Figure 6.4.   The "high wrist" position at a keyboard

OTHER CAUSES

A variety of nonmusical causes also may produce nerve compression problems. The median nerve seems to be affected more commonly than others in this regard, whether due to repetitive forces or to other mechanisms. Any occupation or activity that requires persistent or repeated, forceful wrist flexion may put the user at risk for the development of carpal tunnel syndrome. These work conditions are associated most often with computer or keypunch operators, supermarket checkers, and meat cutters.

Carpal tunnel symptoms also may be caused by a number of nonoccupational conditions. A common cause is the retention of fluid that frequently occurs in women during their last three months of pregnancy. The pressure of this fluid in the unyielding space located at the front of the wrist (the carpal tunnel) can produce median nerve compression. Symptoms usually vanish rather quickly after giving birth when the fluid dissipates. In addition, carpal tunnel syndrome may occur in about one-fifth of patients afflicted with rheumatoid arthritis. Rheumatoid arthritis causes inflammation and thickening of the coverings around the nine tendons that accompany the median nerve through its tunnel. Since the confines of the tunnel are unyielding and cannot expand, the excess bulk of this inflamed tissue creates pressure on the median nerve.

THE MUSICIAN'S ROLE AS PATIENT

How does one know what's *really* going on when nerves are compressed? Here are a few general suggestions for the musician and music teacher to consider. First of all, be alert for the symptoms I have described; they're usually quite specific for nerve problems. Don't ignore or deny them, because procrastination in seeking treatment may lead to permanent nerve and muscle damage and can result in the loss of specialized hand functions. Be aware of the activities and changes in your life that may cause repetitive nerve pressure or overuse of a hand or any other part of the upper extremity. Ask yourself these questions: Have your patterns of hand or arm use changed for any reason? Has a new job, sport, or instrument entered your life, requiring significant changes in postures or activities? In addition, try to determine whether any alterations in your posture or muscle use or other factors make your symptoms better or worse.

Finally, seek professional diagnosis and advice! Those who have studied the body and its medical problems should be your first line of defense against the possibility of serious nerve damage. The family practitioner, internist, neurologist, hand surgeon, and orthopedist are skilled in evaluating and caring for these difficulties. They usually perform a detailed history as well as a physical examination with emphasis on the troubled area, including special nerve tests; sensation, strength, position awareness, and other factors usually are included in this evaluation. In addition, they may request specialized electrical testing of the nerves and muscles to determine the precise site and degree of nerve impingement. This procedure is known as an *EMG/NCV* test and is performed by a trained specialist (a neurologist, neurophysiologist, hand therapist, or physical medicine specialist) who reports the results to the referring physician.

TREATMENT PRINCIPLES

The choice of treatment for this group of problems depends on a number of factors, including the exact location, cause, and severity of the nerve compression. By and large, most types of primary treatment are conservative in nature and are based upon several basic principles.

Activity modification is the primary method of conservative treatment; it helps to decrease or eliminate the physical compression on the nerve. If the activities that produce nerve pressure can be identified precisely, it is quite easy to devise various strategies to avoid them. Even if strict avoidance is not possible, less stringent modifications, such as changing the amount of time spent in troublesome postures or on such causative activities, can be quite helpful. *Exercises* for weak muscles or problem postures also can be beneficial, especially when treating thoracic outlet syndrome.

Splinting the affected body areas during rest or daily activities may help decrease pressure on troubled nerves. Soft, supportive neck collars can be beneficial in treating arthritic problems by providing immobilization to facilitate the relief of inflammation. A wrist splint (figure 6.5) commonly is prescribed for carpal tunnel and other local nerve compressions. Using it prevents the wearer from assuming the postures and positions that can lead to greater nerve damage. Even the elbow can benefit occasionally from a

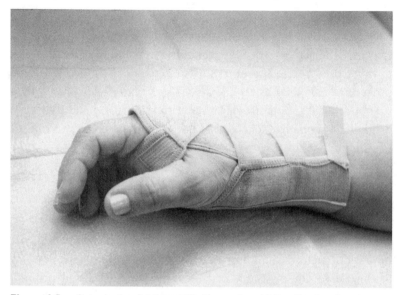

Figure 6.5. **A typical wrist brace limits motion while allowing freedom to the fingers.**

splint designed to minimize repetitive motions or direct pressure on the ulnar nerve.

The physician also may prescribe various *medications* designed to decrease local inflammation about the nerves, thus decreasing the pain and numbness that the patient experiences. Nonsteroidal (noncortisone) medications taken by mouth can minimize inflammation in many areas of the body, including the neck, elbow, and hand. The doctor may elect to inject a locally acting steroid into the area of pressure (but *not* into the nerve itself). This procedure can provide dramatic relief of swelling around the nerve in selected cases, such as in carpal tunnel syndrome with acute swelling and inflammation around the nerve. Any of these treatments usually are accompanied by activity modifications and splinting of the affected area.

If the treatment techniques I've described fail to adequately relieve the nerve pressure and its symptoms, *surgical decompression* of the affected nerve ultimately may be necessary. I've found over the years that such treatment is only required in a minority of cases—most patients can be helped satisfactorily by nonoperative methods. It must be mentioned, though, that the results of surgery, when it is indicated, usually are quite gratifying; the vast majority of these patients are able to return to effective musical perform-ance in a matter of a few weeks. My own medical experience, as well as that of most others, has shown that carpal tunnel syndrome and ulnar nerve compression at the elbow are the two nerve con-ditions most likely to require surgical treatment.

Surgery for these conditions is often recommended as the initial form of treatment in patients with severely compressed nerves, those who show evidence of nerve damage at the time of the first visit. A person with such a serious degree of nerve pressure may not have a chance of good recovery without timely surgical intervention.

The specifics of operative care and the techniques employed vary with the surgeon, the specific nerve, and the cause and location of its compression. These details should be explained thoroughly by the surgeon who would perform the procedure. This person may be a hand or upper extremity surgeon, an orthopedist, or a neurosur-geon or plastic surgeon who is experienced in peripheral nerve re-leases. The procedure can be done in an outpatient setting under local or regional anesthetic and normally takes less than a half hour. Depending on the surgeon's preference, the decompression may be done by traditional open techniques that permit the surgeon to see the nerve and verify its complete release or by endoscopic tech-niques using smaller incisions and usually allowing the patient to re-turn to activities a couple of weeks sooner. In all cases, however, fin-ger movements can (and should) be started immediately after the surgery, and a special surgical dressing may even permit a partial re-turn to music within a week.

Obviously, every patient who is considering surgery must discuss thoroughly all aspects of the procedure, recovery, and rehabilita-tion with the surgeon before making a decision. From my personal experience, I can say that carpal tunnel release has been one of the most gratifying operations I have performed; recovery in more than 90 percent of my patients has been rapid and complete or nearly so, with minimal pain or discomfort and with few people needing prolonged therapy.

Therapy for many nerve injuries can be useful whether or not surgery has been performed. A patient's arm or wrist that has been held in a splint for a prolonged period may benefit from specific exercises designed to restore lost motion, strength, and flexibility. Posture and strengthening exercises for the neck and shoulders are a mainstay of the treatment for thoracic outlet syndrome and other similar conditions, all of which are produced by compression of nerves near the neck vertebrae and upper ribs. In many cases these exercises are carried out under the direction of a physical therapist.

Prolonged rehabilitation is usually not needed for these conditions, but occasionally it can be quite useful after nerve decompression surgery. For the small percentage of patients who have developed some permanent loss of nerve function because of severe or prolonged compression, hand and occupational therapy may help them restore their maximum possible strength, agility, and endurance. Occupational and functional retraining is designed to compensate for losses of both muscle tone and sensory functions and can help such a person cope with the changes required of daily activities as well as musical performance.

SUMMARY

Nerve compression difficulties are quite common, especially those involving the upper extremities. The instrumental musician and teacher must be aware of the causes of, and the symptoms produced by, these nerve compressions; this knowledge is crucial to the effective, early evaluation and treatment of such conditions. Most of these conditions can be treated effectively without resorting to surgery; however, when it's necessary, operative decompression of the nerve offers patients the likelihood of significant recovery of their hand and upper extremity function and can facilitate their return to musical performance.

NOTE

Portions of this chapter were adapted from articles by Dr. William Dawson that appeared in *The Double Reed*, Spring 1992 and Winter 1999; © The International Double Reed Society, Idaho Falls, ID. Reprinted by permission.

SUGGESTIONS FOR FURTHER READING

Dawson, W. J. 1988. Hand and upper extremity problems in musicians: Epidemiology and diagnosis. *Medical Problems of Performing Artists, 3*, 19–22.

Dawson, W. J. 1992. The role of surgery in treating musicians' upper extremity problems. *Medical Problems of Performing Artists, 7*, 56–62.

Dawson, W. J. 1999. Carpal tunnel syndrome: A review of 15 years' clinical experience. *Medical Problems of Performing Artists, 14(1)*, 25–29.

Drew, C. 1988, October 23–26, 30. Cutting corners in the slaughterhouse [Special series]. *Chicago Tribune.*

Lederman, R. J. 1986. Nerve entrapment syndromes in instrumental musicians. *Medical Problems of Performing Artists, 1*, 45–48.

Lederman, R. J. 1989. Peripheral nerve disorders in instrumentalists. *Annals of Neurology, 26*, 640–46.

Roos, D. B. 1986. Thoracic outlet syndromes: Symptoms, diagnosis, anatomy and surgical treatment. *Medical Problems of Performing Artists, 1*, 90–93.

7

ARTHRITIS AND OTHER PROBLEMS OF THE MATURE MUSICIAN

Making music is a lifelong activity and love for most of us. Unlike many other occupations, an instrumental performing career may last as long as seventy years! However, it is a fact that our physical and mental capabilities are subject to change with advancing age. Many of these changes are normal and should be expected, while others are abnormal and are classified as diseases or pathological problems. How, then, can we deal effectively with these changes and yet continue to perform for as long as possible? My purpose in this chapter is to present an overview of some of these age-related conditions as they pertain to the instrumentalist and to present some information about basic methods of dealing with them.

THE JOINTS

The musculoskeletal system is a common site for problems that may arise during the advancing years—and many of these problems are accompanied by pain or discomfort. Foremost among the problems is *osteoarthritis*, a disease characterized by degenerative

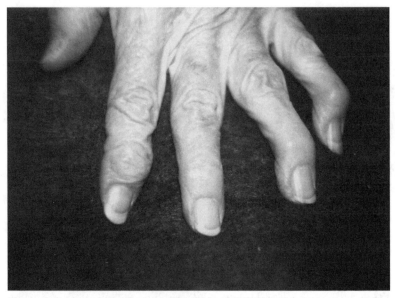

Figure 7.1.   Fingers affected with osteoarthritis; thickenings at the outer joints are called *Heberden's nodes*.

joint changes and also known as "wear and tear" arthritis. Estimates indicate that about 75 percent of people in their seventies develop significant degenerative changes in the smooth, gliding cartilage surfaces of their joints.

The usual spectrum of arthritic symptoms may include: (1) a feeling of *stiffness* about the affected joint, which often feels worse in the morning or after not using the joint for a period of time; (2) *pain*, which most patients describe as dull and aching in character, and which may be aggravated by motion and relieved by rest; and (3) some *loss of joint motion*, usually occurring later in the course of the disease and in many cases accompanied by a relative decrease in the severity of joint pain.

Areas of the body that are of specific concern to musicians and are affected commonly by osteoarthritis include the spine (both the neck and low back), hands, and fingers. People often experience some stiffness and discomfort during or after using their

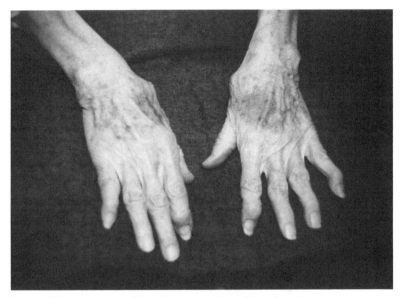

Figure 7.2.   Osteoarthritis of the base joint of the thumb

hands for rapid, repetitive, or forceful motions. Bony spurs or other irregularities around the edges of a joint may develop, producing the thickenings or "knobs" frequently seen on the finger joints nearest the fingernails (figure 7.1).

Increasing damage to those joint surfaces may cause loss or erosion of the underlying bone, thereby making the outermost joint unstable and causing it to deviate to one side; this deformity has obvious implications for instrumentalists as they attempt to cover tone holes on the flute, clarinet, oboe, and bassoon or move along strings in a precise and fluid manner. Women are especially likely to develop these osteoarthritic changes at the bottom joint of their thumbs, where the thumb joins the small bones of the wrist (figure 7.2).

These changes frequently result in stiffness, decreasing the ability to move the thumb away from the palm and the other fingers. This stiffness limits the spread or span of the whole hand, which is needed to play an octave on a piano or grasp a large object. The outermost knuckle of the thumb often becomes loose and unstable from trying to compensate for the loss of movement in the lower joint. All these physical changes are intensified by excess physical stress on the digits, and they can be especially troublesome for the performer who is trying to support an instrument such as the oboe or clarinet or attempting to hold any large or heavy item. Unlike the fingers, the wrist joints are affected much less frequently by these degenerative changes. The motions of wrist flexion and extension, and of forearm rotation, usually are preserved; most people may remain relatively comfortable during the majority of everyday activities, including musical practice and performance.

Stiffness of the spine arising from osteoarthritis may limit one's general flexibility, resulting in difficulty when trying to turn the head from one side to another or to lift it up (and thus watch the conductor). Low back pain and stiffness can make sitting on certain chairs a chore, as well as limiting the length of comfortable sitting time. Occasionally, arthritic spurs on the vertebrae grow large enough to compress a spinal nerve. Since arthritis may affect vertebrae at any level of the spine, compression may occur anywhere from the neck to the low back.

Symptoms of spinal nerve compression usually include shooting pains that travel down one's arm or leg, and often they may be accompanied by feelings of numbness, tingling, or muscle weakness in the affected limb. Decreased sensation or loss of muscle strength are more worrisome symptoms, since they are signs of a more severe condition that ultimately may progress to disabling changes; under these circumstances, early medical evaluation is mandatory to deal with this type of arthritic complication.

The choice of treatment for degenerative joint disease usually depends on the specific joint involved, the severity of damage, the degree of pain and other symptoms experienced by the patient, and how much the process limits everyday activities. As holds true for all the conditions I've mentioned in this chapter, beginning any treatment method should be undertaken only under the direction of a qualified medical professional. Treatment options may include the use of aspirin or some other anti-inflammatory drug, splints for temporary protection of a painful joint, exercises to maintain joint flexibility and muscle strength, local injections of steroids to reduce inflammation, and even an occasional reconstructive surgical procedure.

Although surgery for arthritis often has been considered as a last resort in treatment, it can restore comfort to the patient, as well as permitting increased movement and improved function to a hopelessly damaged joint. One good example of reconstructive surgery is total joint replacement, performed most often on arthritic hips and knees but occasionally on other joints as well. An arthritic hand also may benefit from various reconstructive surgical operations. For instance, stabilizing a loose, painful finger joint by "fusing" or stiffening the adjacent bones to one another in a functional position may allow more firm and comfortable use of that digit. Removal of one of the small bones at the thumb side of the wrist, if it is severely arthritic, often can restore painless movement to a previously sore, stiff thumb.

OTHER CONDITIONS

A special type of bony change, seen most often in women, is *osteoporosis*. Some people's bones lose their normal density and become more porous after menopause, a time that also may be accompanied by a decreased level of physical activity. This bony change is seen most commonly in women of northern European descent and much less commonly in Asians and African Americans. Men also can develop this condition, but it usually begins at a later age. Only 20 percent of osteoporosis occurs in men, but it follows the same genetic and racial patterns as in women. It is not related to arthritis of any kind, nor is it caused by arthritis; however, the two conditions often occur simultaneously.

Osteoporotic bones are more easily fractured (broken), and even a simple slip or a minimal fall may produce a significant injury in the wrist, shoulder, pelvis, or hip or cause a compression-type fracture of a spinal vertebra. Even our physically upright lifestyle may be a source of pain in people affected by osteoporosis. *Micro-fractures* can occur in the spine or pelvis without any specific injury; if the osteoporosis is severe, even some usual vertical activities may be stressful enough to cause compression. These fractures may produce that so-called "dowager's hump" or bent-over, deformed posture that is common in some elderly people.

Since we cannot change our genetic makeup, the prevention and treatment of osteoporosis, especially in women, become the most logical alternatives. The success of both of these programs depends especially upon obtaining good medical advice and pursuing a continuing exercise program that produces vigorous and repetitive muscle pull on the bones, encouraging them to stay dense and strong. In the past decade, a prescription medication that can retard and reverse the bone loss of osteoporosis has become available; its use requires close medical supervision and testing. In addition, using calcium pills and estrogen supplements may be advocated for many women, but these should be taken only on the recommendation of a medical physician who knows the patient and her specific condition and needs.

Other wear-and-tear changes can affect various soft tissues in the body; a commonly involved location is the rotator cuff tendons at the shoulder. This condition is known as *degenerative tendinitis* and produces pain when the shoulder is moved actively, usually while lifting the arm forward or sideways, away from the body. Supporting one's instrument, especially a violin, viola, flute, trumpet, or trombone, can become a painful, difficult chore for those afflicted with this condition.

Treatment of this type of tendinitis usually is conservative in nature and may include the short-term use of medications, in addition to a period of rest to decrease temporarily the physical stress on the shoulder muscles. The musician affected by this condition usually is taught the use of correct body mechanics in order to prevent further damage to these tissues and to minimize muscle strain and its resulting pain. Corrective or adaptive playing techniques, specific for a particular musical instrument, often can be taught by the music teacher, while more general instructions are usually given by a physical therapist. A general recommendation that may be useful is to keep the elbows closer to the body while supporting or playing an instrument. Lifting them outward or away uses more shoulder muscles, and, over the years, repetitive use of this nature may predispose a musician to increased risk of rotator cuff tendinitis or degeneration.

Another condition associated with maturity, and one that can be particularly damaging to an instrumentalist's hand, is *Dupuytren's contracture*. A thickening and tightening of the connective tissues in the palm and fingers characterize this disease. We don't know its basic cause, but it occurs most commonly in people of northern European ancestry and is often associated with various other diseases and conditions. Men are affected more frequently than women, but both can develop such severe tightness of the affected tissues that the hand and fingers cannot open or extend straight out, nor can the fingers spread apart completely (figure 7.3). The little and ring fingers are affected most often—obviously a distressing situation for string players, pianists, and those wind musicians who must operate multiple keys with their small fingers. Dupuytren's disease usually is not painful, and it often takes many years for the condition to develop into a full-blown contracture that limits hand function significantly. Many noninstrumentalists barely notice the gradually increasing limitation in their hand movements and functions until the disease is far advanced. Only surgical removal of the

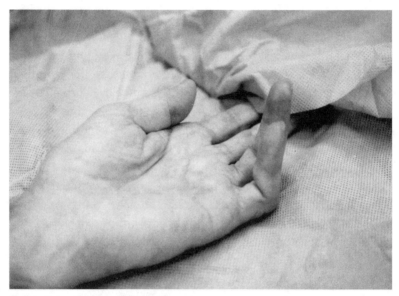

Figure 7.3. Dupuytren's contracture

abnormal connective tissues can restore flexibility to the hand. The tendons, nerves, and blood vessels are spared during this type of operation, but most patients still require a rather long period of rehabilitation to regain good hand function and return to their musical activities.

SPECIAL SENSES

Our *special senses* include sight, hearing, and taste. The first two are particularly important to the performer, since both of them not only lose some of their acuity with advancing age but also may be affected by a number of performance-related difficulties. Science and technology have not as yet developed artificial replacements for our eyes and ears; therefore, it is crucial that we do everything possible to preserve and protect them ("one pair to a customer").

Vision

Most people develop a condition called *presbyopia*, or aging of their vision, sometime during their lives. The first warning signal may be a gradual decrease in the clarity of near vision (up to twenty-four inches away from the eyes), and most of those affected notice it in their early forties. In presbyopia, the small muscles within the eyeball become weaker and cannot adjust the shape of the lens to accommodate seeing objects (including the printed note) at relatively close range. This explains why many people over age forty must wear reading glasses or "bifocals" to see clearly at distances of eighteen to twenty-four inches.

A second age-related change of importance to musicians is a decrease in the acuity of midrange vision. This condition becomes apparent when one looks at objects in the twenty-four- to thirty-six-inch range, the approximate distance from the eyes to the music stand. An additional lens correction may be necessary to allow clear vision at these distances, thus giving rise to the term "trifocals" for those spectacles that incorporate all three levels of visual correction: near, midrange, and distance.

Many optical technicians are skilled at crafting spectacles for people with special visual needs—including making lenses with a large near- or midrange segment at the bottom for reading music and a smaller segment at the top to correct distance vision (enabling them to see the conductor clearly).

Some eyes may develop cloudiness in the lens, that crystalline structure that collects and focuses the light as it enters the eye. This condition is called a *cataract*, and studies have shown that almost every person over the age of seventy-five develops some clouding of the lens in at least one eye. The decrease in vision produced by a cataract usually gets worse gradually and often requires no treatment for many months or years. However, when the loss of vision becomes significant and interferes with everyday life, surgical removal of the cloudy lens (often accompanied by immediate replacement with an artificial substitute lens) may be necessary.

Yet another eye condition that can occur with increasing age is *glaucoma*. The eye contains a clear fluid in the chamber located between the cornea at the front of the eyeball and the lens in the middle. When the pressure of this fluid increases abnormally, a person sees objects less clearly and often may see a "halo" around lights or other bright objects. Like a cataract, glaucoma usually is painless and often is first diagnosed during a professional eye examination. Medicated eye drops can help most patients control the progression of the glaucoma, and surgery usually is not necessary. However, daily medication usually must be continued throughout one's life, and regular eye examinations are mandatory to assure that the condition is kept under good control.

Hearing

Like eyesight, hearing tends to decrease with advancing age. This condition, called *presbyacusis,* should not be confused with the problem *of noise-induced hearing loss (NIHL)*. Noise-induced losses, by contrast, often begin earlier in life and are caused by prolonged or recurrent exposure to abnormally loud noises. I discuss this in greater detail in chapter 11.

Two varieties of hearing loss are age-related: one affects the middle portion of the ear, while the other causes problems in the inner ear and the hearing nerve. The former type, called a *conductive loss*, comes on gradually, usually after age fifty to fifty-five; it affects the transmission of sound in the outer portion of our hearing apparatus, where sounds are gathered and then conducted to the inner, neurological part. The high tones, above 8000 Hz, are affected first, and losses gradually increase in severity to include lower-pitched tones as well. Both ears are usually involved, and the problem can be helped with hearing aids. In a few people this type of hearing loss is caused by stiffening of the joints between the small bones in the middle ear. This produces a loss of motion among the bones and results in a failure to transmit sound properly. Special surgery can help in severe cases of this condition (*oto-sclerosis*).

A more serious type of age-related hearing loss affects the hearing nerve and the inner ear, where the sound waves are changed into nerve impulses, then sent to the brain to be processed. This type is called *sensorineural loss*, or "nerve deafness." The range of decreased tones is also above 6000–8000 Hz, and the condition is permanent. Unlike conduction losses, sensorineural changes cannot be treated with common types of hearing aids. The same inner area of the ear also is affected by NIHL, a condition that affects lower hearing ranges that worsens with age and continued exposure to loud sound levels. Treating these hearing problems is difficult, and hearing aids usually afford only partial relief. Prevention remains the best option.

Dental and Embouchure Changes

Changes of the facial structures with age are common in musicians and nonmusicians alike. However, instrumentalists may feel the impact of these changes much more keenly because they have the potential to affect one's playing (and perhaps one's career). Although wind musicians have the highest degree of risk, players of upper strings (violin and viola) also can suffer from the effects of these problems.

For some musicians, a lifetime of pressure on the teeth from an instrument mouthpiece or reed can produce gradual changes in the position of the teeth in the upper and lower jawbones. These changes in one's dental *occlusion* are gradual, but with the passage of time they may alter the normal embouchure enough to interfere with sound production. In addition, chronic changes in occlusion and bite may lead to the abnormal wearing down of some teeth.

Poor dental hygiene can result in diseases of both teeth and gums. Chronic gum and tooth socket infections (known as *gingivitis* and *periodontitis*, respectively) may cause loosening of the teeth or erosion of the jawbones and ultimately require surgical repair or removal of teeth. Dentures and bridges may restore more normal facial contours and bite, but for the wind instrumentalist both the disease and the treatment can create serious difficulties in playing.

Wear-and-tear changes also can occur in the temporomandibular joints (TMJ), where the lower jaw joins the upper and has its pivot for movements. The two bony surfaces in these joints are separated by a flat plate of fibrous cartilage, which facilitates motions of the lower jaw in multiple directions. Degeneration of this cartilage and of the adjacent joint surfaces often is a result of long-term pressure, such as that produced by chronic tensing of the jaw muscles or grinding of the teeth (*bruxism*).

Abnormal jaw postures are not uncommon during playing of violin or viola, and prolonged side-to-side stressing of the joint "out of position" also can produce degenerative changes in the surfaces. A wide variety of symptoms accompany TMJ problems; the most common ones are clicking and discomfort, felt just in front of the ears. Overuse or misuse activities also may result in TMJ dysfunction, although this problem is seen more frequently in younger players. To maintain a natural jaw posture, the head, neck, and shoulders should maintain a normal postural alignment by bringing the instrument to the player, not vice versa. Choosing proper-sized chin and shoulder rests can help achieve this and will minimize forces on the jaw from trying to hold the instrument with the lower jaw.

Frequent dental examinations offer the best chance for early diagnosis and treatment of facial and dental problems. The spectrum of treatment options for these conditions is extensive. It helps to bring the instrument to the dental appointment to demonstrate the embouchure for the dentist.

COPING MECHANISMS

Lest the reader begins to think that these aging processes are destined to produce a life of pain, stiffness, poor hearing and vision, and loss of musical capabilities in the instrumentalist, a few words of optimism are in order. First, not everyone experiences these conditions to the same degree as others; the extent of individual involvement is extremely variable. It's also unlikely that a person will develop every one of the aging problems I've mentioned, nor develop them at the same age that others do. A lot depends on the way one's parents fared with similar disorders of aging, since many of these conditions have some familial tendencies relating to the time of onset, pattern of disease, and degree of severity.

Second, the advances of medical science have made dealing with the problems of aging much less onerous for many people. I've already alluded to several possible treatment options for these difficulties, but the musician's own medical professional still remains the best source of accurate information on handling these (and all other) health issues.

Regular medical evaluation, coupled with one's willingness to candidly describe all new or ongoing symptoms and problems, can afford each musician the best possible chance to identify a problem in its early stages. Beginning timely and appropriate treatment may minimize "the ravages of time." Many instrumentalists have continued to play effectively into their eighties, and it is likely that most of them have experienced one or more of the problems I've mentioned in this and previous chapters. With proper knowledge and appropriate medical help, the mature performer should be able to maintain a quality of musical life that permits continued enjoyment and expertise well beyond the traditional retirement age of sixty-five.

NOTE

Material in this chapter was adapted from articles by Dr. William Dawson that appeared in the *Journal of the International Double Reed Society*, volume 21, July 1993, and in *The Double Reed*, Autumn 1999; © International Double Reed Society, Idaho Falls, ID. Reprinted by permission.

SUGGESTIONS FOR FURTHER READING

Betz, S. 1989. Are you a victim of T.M.J. dysfunction? *The Clarinet,* February–March, 44–47.

Dawson, W. J. 1992. The role of surgery in treating musicians' upper extremity problems. *Medical Problems of Performing Artists, 7,* 59–62.

Dawson, W. J. 1997. Common problems of wind instrumentalists. *Medical Problems of Performing Artists, 12(4),* 107–11.

Dawson, W. J. 1999. Upper extremity problems of the mature instrumentalist. *Medical Problems of Performing Artists, 14(2),* 87–92.

Fine, L. 1986. Dental problems in wind instrumentalists. *Cleveland Clinic Quarterly, 53(1),* 3–10.

Sataloff, R. T., A. G. Brandfonbrener, and R. J. Lederman, eds. 1998. *Textbook of Performing Arts Medicine,* 2nd ed. San Diego: Singular Publishing Group.

HAND INJURY (TRAUMA)

THE BASICS

Acute injury to the musician's hand is a subject that has received very little mention in either musical or medical circles over the years, despite its often significant impact upon musical perform- ance. As a hand surgeon and a bassoonist, I've developed what might be called a double-barreled interest in hand injuries of all types, and in this chapter I'll share some of my experiences, find- ings, and suggestions.

In more than forty years of treating musicians of all ages, I have found that nonmusic-related trauma has been the most common cause of their hand and finger difficulties. From 1984 to 1996 I saw and documented nearly 1,400 instrumentalists with hand and other upper extremity problems in my practice; more than half (701) came to me complaining of difficulties caused by such trauma. This group included 276 high-level performers, the majority of whom were professional performers or teachers.

These patients had a wide range of injuries. Ligament sprains, bone fractures, and joint dislocations were the most common diagnoses made in this group and comprised the majority of patient injuries. The bones and joints of the hands and wrists were affected more frequently than any other parts of their upper extremities.

At the very least, these kinds of injuries may be only a minor inconvenience to one's continued performance, but a worst-case scenario conceivably could lead to total disability. The ultimate result of any of these injuries depends on the combined efforts of four people: the musician/patient, the medical specialist who treats the injury, the therapist who assists with recovery and rehabilitation, and the music teacher or coach who guides the instrumentalist in the process of returning to performance. This precise and coordinated collaboration of many people's time, knowledge, and dedication is exemplified best by those individuals who are actively involved in the specialty of performing arts medicine.

CAUSES

A musician's hand can be injured in a variety of ways. About 40 percent of my patients' traumatic problems were sustained during participation in sports; two-thirds of these involved a ball of some type. Basketball, baseball, and softball were the most frequent offenders, followed in descending order by football, volleyball, and soccer. I found that more than half of the musicians with sports injuries were under age twenty-two and were students at the primary, secondary, or college or conservatory level. However, it was surprising to find that one in seven of the sports-playing group was a performing professional. Nearly 40 percent of the sport-related group had sustained various bone fractures, while an equal number had sprained a finger joint. The great majority of student musicians were injured during school-sponsored or organized games, the remainder from casual or "pickup" games.

The second-largest cause of hand and finger injuries was a fall on, or a direct blow to, the hand; nearly one-third of the musicians in my practice were hurt in this manner. Sprains and fractures were the most common diagnoses in this group also. Motor vehicle trauma, household accidents, and work-related incidents caused the remainder of the injuries. These causes produced some of the most serious and long-lasting problems, including a variety of cuts or lacerations, power tool injuries, and chronic neck sprains.

COMMON SYMPTOMS

Instrumentalists who suffered trauma to their hands or upper extremities were likely to experience one or more of the three following symptoms. Heading the list was *pain* in the area that had been injured. The degree of pain varied among the different types of trauma and also from one person to another; it did not necessarily correlate with the extent of damage or with the nature of the long-term result. Even though they complained of some pain, however, most people could move their broken or sprained hand to a certain degree. I have also seen this phenomenon frequently in nonmusicians who suffered the same types of injuries. Perhaps this experience should help put to rest the old saying, "I can still move it, so it must not be broken."

Swelling of the affected area was common but did not occur after all types of injuries. It was not necessarily accompanied by pain at the site of injury, nor did it always limit the amount of motion possible at the nearby joints. The most common locations for swelling were at the finger joints, especially the middle knuckle, and over the back of the hand. Sometimes it was produced by internal bleeding, which often occurred around a broken bone; when this happened, the patient also was aware of some *bruising* or discoloration of the skin overlying the injured area.

A third frequent complaint was *deformity*, which I define here as an abnormal shape or alignment of the hand, fingers, or other body area. Deformities of varying types and degrees were frequently associated with fractures or dislocations, where the alignment of the bone or joint was disrupted, and they usually were quite painful. Some broken fingers had dramatic degrees of deformity, such as an injured digit pointing in a radically abnormal direction or appearing to be "stuck" under an adjacent finger. However, less severe deformities were much more common and often were hidden or minimized by swelling; when this occurred, the true, serious nature of the injury might not have been obvious to the patient at first.

SEEKING CARE

Anybody, even one with medical training, may find it difficult to determine early and accurately the true significance of some of these injuries. A number of them will prove ultimately to be innocuous, while others potentially may be disastrous for the instrumentalist. The presence of severe pain or obvious deformity usually indicates a significant injury has occurred, but a minor amount of tenderness, often without any loss of motion in the joint or finger, may not. In this latter situation, a severe and often disabling fracture or joint injury may be shrugged off as "just a sprain," and the injured person may not obtain appropriate care.

Ideally, the musician must seek out qualified health professionals whose skills include familiarity with the hand and its complexities of structure and function. Orthopedic surgeons, hand surgeons, and others who have obtained such specialized training usually are excellent choices in this regard. An additional source of treatment expertise may be a physician who specializes in performing arts medicine. As mentioned previously, this type of doctor is familiar with musicians' specific problems and needs and also can facilitate an instrumentalist's return to maximum possible performance capability.

Care for the injured hand should begin with the recognition that an injury has occurred, followed by seeking appropriate medical help. An accurate and complete diagnosis of the injury is best done on the day the trauma occurred. Early evaluation may help prevent further injury that might result from continued or improper use of the hand. The examining physician may order one or more specialized tests, including X-rays, bone scans, computerized tomography (CAT) scans, and magnetic resonance imaging (MRI tests), to precisely determine the exact nature and extent of damage.

TREATMENT PRINCIPLES

Treatment for any hand or finger injury always should be specific for the individual and the type of trauma sustained; it also should consider the performer's future functional hand needs. The physician can use many different methods of treatment: immobilization of a sprained ligament by a splint, cast, or other method for a number of days or weeks, depending on the location and severity of the problem; and *reduction* or "setting" of fractured bones and dislocated joints to restore their correct alignment and immobilization to facilitate healing and prevent the return of any deformity. Various splints are used, from a plaster or fiberglass cast wrapped around a broken hand or wrist, to a strip of metal and soft foam taped onto a sprained finger.

Some injuries may require surgical treatment, which is often necessary when there is an open wound or when the injury cannot be treated by other methods or will not stay fixed by splinting alone. Often, surgically stabilizing or "internal splinting" of a fracture with a combination of metal pins, screws, or plates actually may make the bone firm and stable enough to allow some early motion in the injured area while it heals.

Frequently, an operation actually reduces the chances of developing stiffness following the injury and minimizes the severity of any stiffness that develops; surgical treatment also may decrease the time required for full rehabilitation and return to music. A number of injuries require operative repair as the primary and traditional means of treatment. For example, cut nerves and tendons usually must be sewn together so they can heal in as normal a fashion as possible; without this repair, they usually will not be able to function. Most patients with open wounds, including skin lacerations (cuts) and fingertip injuries, must be treated at the time of injury by wound care, suture, or other techniques.

AFTER INJURY

The immediate concern to an instrumentalist with a hand or other upper extremity injury is the amount of time that must be spent away from his or her instrument. Many factors help determine this interval; I have already discussed those relating to the nature of the injury and the musician's decision to seek timely care. Other equally important factors include the quality of medical care and rehabilitation and the extent to which the patient can participate actively in the treating and healing process. In this last regard, I cannot emphasize too strongly the fact that each patient has to become a knowledgeable and willing participant in the entire treatment process in order to achieve the best possible result following trauma or other problems that affect performance.

Long-term effects or complications of hand and other upper extremity injury can pose significant problems for the instrumentalist, as well as for anyone who uses their hands in very precise ways. These effects may be prolonged or permanent and can include such conditions as persistent pain, joint stiffness with loss of motion, deformity of a digit, numbness due to nerve injury, or decreased voluntary movements after tendons have become damaged and scarred. These conditions may be related to the severity of the injury, the timeliness of care, the development of secondary difficulties, the duration and effort of rehabilitation, or many other factors.

Late problems such as these frequently affect the mechanics of playing an instrument; if this should happen, musical technique changes or instrument modifications may become necessary to help regain performance skills. Many other late effects, however, produce chronic and permanent changes that cannot be treated effectively. For these patients, more drastic personal and musical life changes may be the only answer. Some of the musicians I have treated for these long-term problems have had to modify their playing style or their repertoire, and a few of them went on to develop secondary overuse-related syndromes because of these technique changes. Others were forced to change instruments or were able to play only some instruments but not others. All but three of the nearly three hundred high-level musicians in my practice who suffered hand or upper extremity trauma were able to return to some manner of musical performance.

A case in point is that of a musician in her forties who broke her left wrist in a fall; the bones healed well, but because of stiffness she was unable to fully rotate her forearm and wrist into a palm-down position (*pronation*). Two years after the injury she was unable to play the piano with this hand but still could rotate her wrist enough to play the flute. In only a few severe cases, patients were forced to give up playing music altogether because of a permanent disability following injury.

SOME GUIDELINES

Here are a few guidelines that may be helpful, either in preventing an injury or getting the best possible final result if one should occur:

1. "Spring training" for the hands is important when resuming any sport involving a ball. I've found that most injuries sustained

while playing these sports were caused by catching the ball with the hands in the wrong position, and the majority of these occurred early in the season, before the athlete had regained sports-specific skills.

2. Wear protective equipment, correctly sized and appropriate to each sport, for all practices and games. Although it's nearly inconceivable to think that a symphony musician would play a pickup game of softball barehanded during summer festival rehearsals, I know it has happened—and more than once!

3. Recognize that pain is a warning signal given to us by our bodies when something is wrong; heed it by stopping the painful activities and resting the injured area.

4. Seek early, expert care for any problem or injury involving your hands and fingers (as well as for all parts of your body). Don't try to "play through" the pain and hope it will go away. What you do in the first few hours or days after an injury usually will play a major role in determining how well you will recover later.

5. Not every injured hand can be restored to "normal," but I have found that most patients who have sustained these types of trauma can return to effective music performance. However, it often takes a lot of time and the combined efforts of the musician/patient, physician, therapist, and teacher to achieve this result.

NOTE

Material contained in this chapter was adapted from an article by Dr. William Dawson that appeared in *The Double Reed*, Fall 1991; © The International Double Reed Society, Idaho Falls, ID. Reprinted by permission.

SUGGESTIONS FOR FURTHER READING

Crabb, D. J. M. 1980. Hand injuries in professional musicians. *The Hand, 12(2)*, 200–208.

Dawson, W. J. 1992. The role of surgery in treating musicians' upper extremity problems. *Medical Problems of Performing Artists, 7*, 59–62.

Dawson, W. J. 1995. Experience with hand and upper extremity problems in 1,000 instrumentalists. *Medical Problems of Performing Artists, 10(4)*, 128–33.

Dawson, W. J. 1996. Hand and upper extremity trauma in high-level instrumentalists: Epidemiology and outcomes. *Work, 7*, 81–87.

9

TREATMENT ALTERNATIVES

Just as there are many "correct" ways to play a musical phrase, a variety of methods is available to treat many medical conditions faced by the instrumentalist. A health professional prescribes or administers some of these methods, and the patient may purchase many others directly (over the counter). Many options exist because they all do the job in one way or another and because health professionals do not agree on a single effective remedy. In addition, different people respond differently to any one type of treatment.

In the same fashion, many different types of practitioners treat musicians' problems. Some fall within the category of so-called traditional medicine, while others adhere to a variety of nontraditional principles and philosophies. In our increasingly health-conscious society, patients are taking a greater personal initiative in learning about health-care options and making their own decisions regarding care. I have included this chapter to help the instrumentalist make such choices, as well as for the following additional reasons:

1. For many years, performing artists have routinely obtained much of their health care from different types of non-MD

practitioners. Prior to the emergence of performing arts medicine, few doctors were aware of the special needs of performers and lacked the special knowledge and skills to treat them effectively. Some patients became distrustful of traditional medicine and sought out those nontraditional practitioners who would spend greater periods of time evaluating their symptoms and lifestyle, as well as deliver more of their treatment in a hands-on fashion.

2. Some musicians may feel they have obtained less than optimum results from traditional treatment methods and are seeking more effective care for their problems. This group needs to know that additional treatment options do exist; they also deserve factual information on the philosophies of these methods, how such alternatives can help them, and what each one's limitations are.

3. Millions of people around the world use nontraditional healing techniques for their health problems and have done so for thousands of years. Our libraries and bookstores are full of self-help books on these subjects. Print and broadcast media bombard us daily with advertisements for a wide range of medicines, food supplements, and devices. Alternative health-care costs range in the billions of dollars (as well as in yen, Euros, pounds, and other currencies) annually.

4. Finally, I wish to present a concept that both traditional and nontraditional methods of health care can coexist effectively for the benefit of patients troubled with a wide variety of difficulties. This concept is neither new nor unique; in addition, adherents of any single philosophy of treatment should not consider it as radical or heretical.

WHAT IS "NONTRADITIONAL"?

Rather than define nontraditional methods, I will describe them using examples or contrast their methods with those of traditional medicine. Traditional medical approaches include care by both allopathic (MD) and osteopathic (DO) physicians, as well as by physical and occupational therapists who work under their direction and prescription.

Many nontraditional (also called alternative, complementary, or integrative) treatment disciplines are not grounded in scientific principles or methods like traditional treatments. Often, they rely more on faith and individual experience and on beliefs that powers existing outside or beyond the natural world affect the course of some events and present little "hard" scientific data to back up their claims. However, many alternative methods address desirable treatment goals, namely, peace of mind, happiness, and quality of life. Some alternative health disciplines emphasize the use of *natural healing;* however, they do not seem to be related to the well-known physiological processes by which a living organism tends to heal itself (e.g., from injury). Often, alternative treatment disciplines rely heavily on the placebo effect (the relief or lessening of symptoms after taking medication with no active ingredients—a "sugar pill"). Although some patients may notice improvement after such alternative treatments, I cannot recommend them for life-threatening situations.

LESS-THAN-HONEST PRACTITIONERS

For nontraditional practitioners who are not licensed by governmental bodies, it can be difficult to differentiate a well-trained person from an opportunist or outright charlatan. Beware of the following practices or claims:

1. Promises that a method or drug will *cure* a *variety* of ailments *quickly.*
2. The use of case histories or testimonials to bolster claims.
3. Claims of a "secret" or "special" ingredient or formula.
4. Statements defaming or condemning the medical establishment.

TYPES OF ALTERNATIVE CARE

The following section is not meant to be a comprehensive or exhaustive review of available nontraditional treatment methods but rather a short description of some disciplines that may be useful to the instrumentalist or others unfamiliar with their various philosophies of disease and treatment. For the sake of convenience, I have grouped them arbitrarily into six categories: manual therapy, topical therapy, body awareness methods, acupuncture, dietary therapy, and homeopathy. However, not all methods in a single group may share similar philosophies.

Manual Therapy

Physical Therapy.   Many states now allow registered physical therapists to diagnose and treat patients without a physician's referral. The nature and quality of care these patients receive is no different from that given to a referred patient, but individual therapists differ in their diagnostic and treatment skills. I consider physical therapy to be an alternative form of care only when it does not involve a physician and when it relies on patient self-referral to the therapist (which may or may not be the optimal choice for a particular problem).

Massage Therapy.   Massage therapists are licensed in many states but are not required to undergo the same rigorous training program as a physical therapist. Therapeutic massage can be very effective for a variety of muscle problems, as well as affording the recipient a feeling of relaxation and well-being at the completion of a treatment session. In some cases, patients prefer a massage therapist to a physical therapist for muscular difficulties, and physician referrals to this specialty are increasing.

Chiropractic.   The United States has more than fifty thousand licensed chiropractic physicians. The founder of chiropractic, Daniel Palmer, believed that all illnesses or physical impairments are caused by out-of-line vertebrae ("subluxations") that create pressure on spinal nerves and interfere with the function of the organs supplied by those nerves. He recommended treatment that involves manual "adjustment" of the vertebrae to relieve the subluxation. This definition of subluxation is peculiar to chiropractic thought and is not shared by osteopathic physicians and MDs.

Chiropractic began about one hundred years ago as a single philosophy of disease and treatment, but in the succeeding years it has branched out to include wider concepts. Three types of practitioners currently work in this field: (1) The "straights" continue to follow the philosophies and precepts originally set down by the founder. (2) The "mixers" share Palmer's beliefs that mechanical disturbances of the nervous system are fundamental, but they also recognize other causes of disease. Their treatment spectrum includes adjustments but also encompasses massage, ultrasound, and other physical modalities, as well as advice on general lifestyle, health, and nutrition. (3) A third group limits itself to the diagnosis and treatment of nonsurgical neuromuscular and musculoskeletal disorders. This form of chiropractic is newer, and its system of beliefs differs even more from Palmer's than that of the mixers. All three groups of chiropractors cannot legally write traditional drug prescriptions, and therefore they limit their treatment to physical methods and (for some practitioners) nonprescription dietary aids and supplements.

Topical Therapy

Applying substances to the skin for relief of various conditions is a long-standing part of both traditional and alternative medicine, as well as of sports training and health care. A variety of chemicals act as local skin irritants and actually can cause increased blood circulation at and near the skin, with increased surface heat. Some people believe that applying salicylates (aspirin-like compounds) over inflamed or painful deep tissues relieves local inflammation and decreases the associated symptoms. A physical therapy modality known as *phonophoresis* uses steroid compounds (similar to cortisone) with local ultrasound to facilitate the absorption of the drug through the skin. When the steroids are combined with low-dose electrical current, the modality is called *iontophoresis,* and the results are similar.

For more than forty years, people have used an industrial compound called dimethylsulfoxide (DMSO) to relieve local pain and inflammation; despite its antioxidant qualities, it is not currently approved by the Food and Drug Administration. Many people have used it nonetheless and have reported great benefit. A major drawback to its use is the resulting garlic-like odor on the user's breath, an obvious indication that the body absorbs the chemical through intact skin and distributes it through the bloodstream.

Body Awareness Methods ("Bodywork")

The Alexander technique, Feldenkrais technique, and yoga are based on rather similar philosophies, despite their vast differences in national origin and years of use. All three treatment practices focus on movement, posture, and meditation, although in somewhat different ways.

Alexander Technique.   More than one hundred years ago the Australian actor Frederick Matthias Alexander was having difficulty in projecting his voice in large theaters. As he discovered techniques to overcome this difficulty, he developed several theories of body awareness and control that are now taught by practitioners trained in these techniques. This discipline's aim is to regain correct spinal alignment and improve the posture of the head, neck, and back; practitioners describe it as an aid to one's physical and psychological well-being and a preventive technique for musculoskeletal problems.

The Alexander practitioner teaches the patient to recognize and "unlearn" established adult patterns of chronic muscle tightness ("spasm") by exercises and gentle manipulation of the head, neck, and body. The patient must participate actively in this process, working to achieve greater levels of body awareness and relaxation. This method has proved helpful to many people suffering from musculoskeletal problems, but not from visceral or internal organ diseases.

Feldenkrais Technique.   A Russian physicist, Moshe Feldenkrais, developed this set of techniques as a way to help his own previously injured knees. His methods are designed to improve the range of body motion and to aid flexibility, coordination, and function. The program has two components: (1) sessions devoted to verbally guided movement awareness, involving thinking, sensing, meditating, and imagining; during these sessions, the patient is taught a variety of body movements; (2) and hands-on sessions devoted to the same set of movements as in the first part but with the addition of guiding and manipulation performed by the licensed practitioner. People claim that it benefits those with neuromuscular disorders, including multiple sclerosis, stroke, spinal injury, and various motor disorders. Practitioners also use it to treat those less seriously afflicted, as well as to retrain the body in proper postures and movements necessary for a variety of occupations and sports.

Yoga.   This is a centuries-old Eastern discipline composed of more than twenty different practices or philosophies. Their common goal is to achieve *nirvana*—that is, enlightenment and complete freedom from tensions. People use yoga as an adjunct to traditional treatments for various neuromuscular disorders to strengthen and relax the body. Three components—postures, breathing, and meditation—are basic to achieving its goals.

1. Exercises designed to achieve and hold specific bodily postures are used to improve circulation, stimulate bodily organs, stretch the body, and restore normal alignment of body structures.

2. Breathing exercises, using controlled and held breaths, accompany the postural exercises.

3. Meditation seeks detachment from the environment by avoiding feelings and emotions to obtain a tranquil, peaceful, and "enlightened" state. I believe that it also can put some people more "in touch" with their bodies and can help them control nonyoga body positions and motor activities more effectively; it also seems to have a relaxing or tension-relieving component.

Acupuncture and Its Variants

For thousands of years, the principles of Chinese medicine, including pulse diagnosis, herbal medicine prescriptions, and insertion of needles along predefined "meridians" or body lines, have been practiced in both Asian and Western countries, and it has a few adherents in the United States today. Needle stimulation, or *acupuncture*, is now a well-recognized treatment modality in and of itself. Trained practitioners of the art, many of them licensed physicians, employ acupuncture as an adjunct to traditional treatment methods.

When properly done, insertion (and, often, manipulation) of sterile, single-use acupuncture needles into certain superficial body areas can control pain and may even relieve some types of pain entirely for the duration of their use. It has been used with generally good effect as an anesthesia for certain surgical procedures, often combined with traditional anesthetic medications. In addition, acupuncture sessions, when used as an adjunct to other treatment modalities, often help people with chronic pain conditions. I have referred patients myself for this treatment, and most of them obtained positive results (but not cures) from the procedures.

Acupuncture can also help treat a number of other conditions. Clinical studies have reported that it is effective in reducing nausea, especially following cancer chemotherapy, and in reducing the frequency and severity of attacks in patients with chronic asthma. Other medical uses, although accompanied by less well-documented success studies, include treatment of drug or alcohol abuse and cessation of smoking. In all the above circumstances, acupuncture has been employed under the direction of a physician and is generally used in combination with other treatment methods.

Acupressure and Shiatsu.   These two derivatives of acupuncture rely on manual pressure on various body areas, not on the insertion of needles. However, the aims of all three philosophies and treatment are quite similar: they claim to increase the flow of "ki" ("qi"), or body energy, as a method of treating various conditions. Each technique employs pressure (acupressure) or massage (Shiatsu) to the same body lines, or meridians, that are recognized in acupuncture.

Reflexology.   This is a comparatively new discipline, although it is based on some of the same five-thousand-year-old Chinese principles I've alluded to earlier. Practitioners apply manual pressure or stimulation to certain "reflex points" (especially the ears, palms of the hands, and soles of the feet) to enhance the flow of the body's "bioelectrical energy" or send impulses by some type of pathway to specific bodily organs. Reflexology practitioners claim their treatment technique is useful in assessing and improving the function of these organs. Some practitioners believe this "flow" operates through the same pathways used in acupuncture; however, little scientific evidence supports these claims. Many people find that a reflexology session leaves them with a feeling of relaxation and well-being, just like a good massage. It's not surprising, therefore, to find that reflexology practitioners are often masseurs, masseuses, or massage therapists as well.

Dietary Therapy

This area of alternative care has become immensely popular in the United States and Europe in the past few decades, resulting in a flood of books and a staggering choice of vitamins, dietary supplements, and herbal remedies. A few dietary plans even have some well-run scientific studies to back up their claims. Briefly put, studies show that some diets, supplements, and herbs are medically useful, and traditional practitioners often recommend them as part of a patient's treatment plan. However, others may be harmful. I recommend Dr. Isadore Rosenfeld's book (see Suggestions for Further Reading) for a good overview of this subject.

Homeopathy

Homeopathy treats the sick with diluted plant and other extracts that in undiluted doses produce similar symptoms in healthy subjects. Practitioners use these extracts to stimulate the body's immune system. Most practitioners would not recommend homeopathy, which often takes weeks to achieve the desired effects, for life-threatening situations or diseases. It may, however, be a viable alternative for less critical conditions with no satisfactory traditional medical treatment or when treatment would be potentially toxic.

THE BEST OF BOTH WORLDS?

During my years of practice, I developed a pragmatic approach to treatment, not only for performing artists but also for patients in general. Based on the principle of "if it works and does not harm, it's good," my treatment options expanded far beyond the traditional philosophies and practices taught in medical school and postgraduate hospital training. From the experience gained by following numerous patients and observing the results of many varieties of care, I developed some personal beliefs about treatment that are worth sharing.

Our bodies try to heal themselves. This is a phrase I've used for more than forty years, and its truth is based on sound physiological principles. Infections wall themselves off, or "come to a head"; fractures can heal without medical care, although the position of the bones may not be ideal. We all possess these natural powers of healing, and all health-care philosophies, traditional or nontraditional, share this belief.

Treatment should employ, enhance, and optimize these natural powers whenever possible. Certainly there will be times when open wounds must be closed surgically, acute diabetic crises must be treated with insulin, and many other similar indications will require the knowledge and skills of a traditional physician. But in many other circumstances, nontraditional methods, or a rational combination of the traditional and the alternative, may indeed be more effective than "establishment medicine" alone. This is where, I believe, the pragmatic approach offers much more than the orthodox, and I encourage both physicians and patients to consider the possible benefits of multiple treatment modalities when the indications are appropriate.

I have two caveats about this philosophy: First, *do no harm.* All methods of treatment must be complementary, not conflicting; each practitioner involved in any type of combined care must be aware of the possible adverse interactions among all the various chemicals and other substances being used in treatment.

Second, each practitioner must know that the patient is receiving other treatment and must be in regular communication with the patient and all other healers. This is easy to do if one practitioner refers the patient directly for additional care from another discipline. However, if the patient makes the decision to obtain additional care, it is his or her responsibility to inform each practitioner of the other's role in the treatment process, and all practitioners must approve of the combined program. Without adequate communication among all concerned parties, it is far too easy for treatment to be prolonged, less than effective, or outright dangerous for the patient.

SUGGESTIONS FOR FURTHER READING

Raso, Jack. 1994. *"Alternative" Healthcare—A Comprehensive Guide.* Amherst, NY: Prometheus Books.

Rosenfeld, Isadore. 1996. *Dr. Rosenfeld's Guide to Alternative Medicine.* New York: Random House.

GETTING BACK TO MUSIC
(REHABILITATION)

THE WHAT AND WHY

Many instrumentalists experience great difficulty in returning to full musical activities after being treated for a problem that has affected their performance. Although the original problem was cured or controlled, they continue to have residual physical limitations that interfere with their return to music. These additional conditions are not really complications of the original problem or its treatment. Rather, they are likely to be caused by one of three related factors:

1. The problem itself may produce physical sequelae or aftereffects that interfere with playing. For instance, a crushing fingertip injury on a person's left hand may result in numbness at the tip, with a decrease in the acute sense of touch that is so critical to playing a stringed instrument. Other injuries, not caused by music, can produce chronic physical changes due to scarring, loss of smooth tendon gliding, joint stiffness or contractures after fractures, or pain at the site of a prior injury.

2. The treatment may be the cause of these limitations. Patients recovering from overuse-related conditions, especially those that involve their hands and upper extremities, often discover that disuse or prolonged therapeutic rest from their usual musical activities has resulted in a diminution of their normal muscle-tendon flexibility, strength, and endurance. The older musician also may become aware of some residual joint stiffness after completing the initial treatment of an overuse-related problem.

3. The time spent away from one's instrument during treatment may produce these limitations. Maintaining precise motor skills such as timing, finger placement, and patterns of hand motions requires frequent and regular practice. For some performers, the loss of physical strength following the period of treatment may interfere with carrying or holding a large instrument or even with prolonged playing of a lighter one (the flute, for example).

Rehabilitation, as used in this book, is the process that addresses these residual physical deficits and restores the performer's physical capacity and function to a degree sufficient to permit returning to musical performance at the highest possible level. It does not always mean restoring all one's capabilities and functions back to normal—or even to a level that existed just prior to the disease or injury. Despite the best efforts of all concerned parties, such a degree of restoration may not be possible. For instance, when a nerve is cut, even the most precise microsurgical repair cannot reconnect all the tiny nerve fibers with total accuracy, and some loss of sensation or motor function is to be expected.

SOME BASIC PRINCIPLES

Rehabilitation is an active process. The patient must understand the need for it as well as the principles and activities necessary to achieve the desired results. Cooperation goes hand in hand with understanding; the patient is expected to follow the prescribed program to its completion and to expend a certain degree of physical and mental effort in the process.

Most musician patients cannot rehabilitate alone; obtaining optimum results requires a combination of professional help, education, and guidance. Traditionally the person responsible for treatment (the physician or equivalent) institutes and supervises the overall process, but a professional therapist usually is in charge of the day-to-day management—including initially evaluating the patient's condition, education, and ongoing monitoring of the results. Practitioners of physical therapy, occupational therapy, and specialized hand therapy have the special training and knowledge of techniques necessary to help restore specific physical capabilities after injury or illness. Some of these therapists are musicians themselves and thus bring to the rehabilitation process the added knowledge of a performer's special functional needs and how to help restore them to the highest possible degree.

The music teacher or coach also plays a most important role in the patient's return to instrumental performance; this is true whether or not the problem was a direct cause of playing music. The teacher often can devise or demonstrate a variety of specialized exercises on the instrument to help regain elements of hand and finger flexibility and dexterity that cannot be achieved by medical means alone. Sometimes it is possible to begin this so-called technique rehabilitation during the medical phase of treatment, thus avoiding any unnecessary delay and minimizing the negative effects of musical inactivity.

Each person who undergoes rehabilitation for a physical problem possesses a unique set of circumstances that the treating team must consider. For this reason, each rehabilitation program is custom tailored for the individual in its nature, intensity, and duration. In many cases, the length of time spent in regaining one's physical capabilities may far exceed the time required to treat the original problem. This situation seems to be especially true for problems involving the musculoskeletal or neurological systems. For example, it takes several times longer to restore muscle strength than it did to lose it. In addition, cut or damaged nerves regenerate at an average rate of one inch per month, so recovery of sensation and muscle function after nerve repair may require many months.

"SPRING TRAINING" FOR THE MUSICIAN

Problems

Treatment of a medical problem often results in a decrease or loss of many different physical capabilities and skills. Some of these changes are obvious in the early stages of the healing process, while others may not be recognized until the patient attempts to resume previously routine activities. Some are quite obvious to both the patient and those around him or her, while others may be subtle and become evident only when performing very precise or complicated movements. Some changes are physical or physiological in nature, while others fall more into the artistic realm.

Several of the physical parameters that may be affected include muscle strength, flexibility of the muscle and its associated tendons, smooth gliding of tendons during motions, endurance (here, the repetition of strength and physical activity), joint flexibility and range of motion, speed or quickness of movements, coordination of motions both large and small, and, after some nerve problems, critical sensation and motor (muscle) functions. For some patients who have been severely injured or ill for long periods, their general health and conditioning likely have been compromised as well.

In the artistic realm, a performer may notice difficulty in precisely placing fingers on keys or strings or in playing some musical passages with the proper timing, coordination, or agility. In addition, endurance for musical practice or performance has suffered;

this limitation affects not only the duration of musical sessions but also the difficulty of repertoire that can be played. Obviously, some of these physical and artistic parameters often overlap, but the musician must recognize that both are involved and closely related. The chosen methods of rehabilitation must address both areas of limitations.

Solutions

For the instrumentalist, the wide spectrum of possible rehabilitation modalities or techniques can be arranged into four useful categories: exercises, motor skills, sensory training, and musical rehabilitation. The degree of emphasis to be placed on each category, as well as the choice of techniques, depends on the person involved and his or her specific condition and needs. As I mentioned earlier, each program should be geared to the needs of the individual and be supervised by a trained health professional.

Exercise programs come in many varieties, each with its own set of indications, methods, and expected results. *Isometric* or *isotonic* muscle exercises improve strength and endurance. In the former method, the muscle maintains a constant length during a contraction without movement in the adjacent joints. By contrast, the latter method maintains a constant degree of muscle tension while the joint is moved through a range of motion. All muscles can be exercised in both ways.

A special technique known as *isokinetic* exercise improves muscle endurance. In this method, the patient uses one or more types of exercise machines that provide varying combinations of speed and power during muscle contractions. Exercises on other machines can restore functional movement patterns, so necessary for all of life's activities. These machines duplicate and guide specific combinations of movements; this form of therapy has been used with great effect in occupational rehabilitation as an efficient way to restore specific job skills.

A program of stretching and flexibility exercises is helpful in treating stiff muscles and tight or "stuck" tendons. It is necessary to restore a full range of muscle movement (by contraction and relaxation) so that the muscles can use their full power in all ranges of movement, as well as to allow full motion of normal joints.

Loss of normal tendon gliding is common after immobilizing an arm or leg for, say, a broken bone or after surgical treatment of various extremity problems. The early use of specific exercises can help preserve or improve this critical activity; in general, the results of such exercise programs are not as good if they are begun late in the course of rehabilitation.

Like muscles, joints can become stiff or lose some of their mobility following various treatment programs. Immobilization of a joint causes the soft tissues around it to contract and thus limit its movement; in addition, the cartilage gliding surfaces lose some of their smooth, glistening characteristics that allow comfortable freedom of motion. Exercises are extremely useful in treating such stiff joints, but often they must be continued for many months to achieve satisfactory results.

Motor skills programs are designed to help those patients who, for various reasons, have lost their normal capabilities for rapid and repetitive activities or for precision movements. These programs emphasize coordination and other elements of mental control and are used frequently in the rehabilitation of neurological disorders. An occupational therapist usually administers this type of retraining therapy, since it is designed to help regain the gross and fine motor functions needed for specific activities or occupations.

Sensory reeducation is another modality used by the occupational therapist. This process, like motor skills retraining, employs highly specialized learning techniques to help people recovering from central or peripheral nerve injuries and other problems. Overly sensitive areas of skin (fingertips, for example) can be desensitized, while patients with sensory losses can learn ways to adapt and modify their activities, thus achieving functional improvement in many of their myriad daily activities.

Musical rehabilitation takes over when the patient's general physical needs are met but when the specific requirements of musical performance still require improvement. As with medical rehabilitation, musical "therapy" can take many forms, depending on the nature of the injury, the instrumentalist's condition, and the specific functions needed in order to return to maximum possible playing capability. At this point in the rehabilitation process, the music teacher or coach assumes the primary role in evaluating the specific deficits, formulating the proper exercise program, and guiding the patient's (student's) progress.

I believe that first and foremost in any musical rehabilitation program is the need to resume correct basic posture while holding and playing the instrument. Whether the musician plays sitting or standing, he or she must follow the principles of correctly aligned posture: the head should be positioned over the center of the shoulders, the spine held as straight as the musician's current anatomical situation allows, and the whole torso centered over the two "sitting bones" of the pelvis (in medical terms, the *ischial tuberosities*). The musician should then bring the instrument to the correctly positioned body, not vice versa, so that the maximum number of unneeded muscles can remain relaxed. Obviously, those muscles that are required to support and play the instrument must be functioning or in a state of readiness, but relaxing all the others permits greater technical facility and minimizes the chance of secondary muscle strain.

Second, the performer's hands and fingers must resume their technically correct and efficient positions on the instrument, whatever its type. It may take a certain amount of relearning or becoming familiar with these postures, but I feel this is essential if one wishes to return to optimum playing. The instrumental teacher can provide assistance in this situation, in much the same fashion as when teaching a brand-new student. Musicians whose injuries have resulted in permanent upper extremity deformities need to learn some degree of modification; for these patients, a perceptive and knowledgeable music teacher can work with physicians and therapists to devise appropriate hand or finger postures, as well as exercises to improve technique under these altered circumstances.

Instrument-based exercise or practice programs can help restore the precise finger placement, control, and coordination needed to play fast or complicated musical passages. Beginning simply and slowly, and progressing to faster and more complex material, these techniques allow the performer to regain many all-important motor skills. As progress continues, increasingly more difficult repertoire becomes possible.

As a patient returns to making music, one of the most important duties a teacher must assume is that of guiding and monitoring the practice schedules and times. It is critical to limit practice times and intensity in the early phase of musical rehabilitation, especially when the initial problem has been caused by overuse activities. Instrumentalists must achieve playing endurance gradually and comfortably, and a knowledgeable and astute teacher can be of great help in achieving this goal. Guidance of this type may help prevent such secondary problems as overcompensation, trying to "make up for lost time" in one's musical life, or backsliding into pain or other symptoms because of using improper musical techniques.

A variety of instrument modifications also may assist in the rehabilitation process. These may be devised by the music teacher, therapist, performer, or someone who makes or repairs instruments. Adaptations may range from the relatively simple to the comparatively complex, yet all are designed to allow the performer to hold the instrument more easily or to reach the keys or strings with less finger movement or effort. I have seen a clarinet with alternate little-finger keys added to relieve one hand of a painful fingering stretch, and (believe it or not!) low D-flat and E-flat keys moved to the left thumb position on a bassoon after the performer's left little finger was paralyzed. Bow handles may be enlarged or reshaped.

Extending or enlarging certain keys on woodwind instruments will enable an unfortunate musician who has lost part of a finger traumatically to resume playing with pre-injury skills. Some instrument modifications may be temporary, needed only during the rehabilitation phase of trauma or overuse problems; others may become permanent if disability continues for a long period of time or if the performer actually finds them more useful or more comfortable than the original configuration.

Breathing exercises may help those wind instrumentalists whose problems have resulted in decreased respiratory capacity or function. Depending on the specific needs, the individual can practice these exercises both with and without the instrument. Choice of the proper techniques can address problems of air pressure, volume, and respiratory endurance.

FROM REHABILITATION TO PREVENTION

This is actually a very small step but an extremely important one. Indeed, it is the central focus of current performing arts medicine thinking and practice. After a medical problem has been resolved by treatment, and after physical skills and musical capabilities have been restored by rehabilitation, the performer should try to avoid any possible recurrences of that problem. After all, why be subjected to another period of discomfort or pain, expense, loss of income (for some), and time away from an important part of one's life, when it may be prevented by some comparatively simple techniques and practices?

Although this section is most specific for those who have experienced overuse-related problems, the same concept of prevention can be applied to traumatic and other conditions as well. In all cases, it requires a conscious effort on the performer's part, as well as a certain amount of desire and discipline, to be successful—just as the rehabilitation process does.

Prevention requires first of all that the musician take a critical backward look at the original problem, identifying its causes and contributing factors. Most of these probably were identified during the early evaluation and treatment phases by the patient, physician, or therapist and confirmed later during the process of musical rehabilitation. They may have ranged from the subtle to the blatantly obvious, but effective prevention depends on fully recognizing them and the roles they played in the initial problem.

The second step the musician must take is to apply the principles of common sense and logic in formulating strategies to avoid these causal activities and modify the factors contributing to the problem. Some of these methods may be as simple as taking a five-minute break from practicing every half hour, or regularly observing one's playing posture in a mirror. In many cases a trial-and-error approach is helpful—for example, a violinist or violist trying various combinations of shoulder pads and chin supports to avoid neck and shoulder strains. The performer's general health is often overlooked as an important element in the prevention process; maintaining proper physical conditioning and capabilities requires a number of nonmusical efforts that I'll mention in the next chapter.

The third phase of prevention is actually putting these changes into effect. The process is not automatic but requires the musician to develop a number of new and more useful habits to ensure that the changes become permanent—a process that takes personal awareness, dedication, time, and effort. The goal is being able to practice and perform comfortably and effectively, without the recurrence of interfering physical difficulties.

SUGGESTIONS FOR FURTHER READING

Bejjani, F. J. 1993. Performing artists' occupational disorders. In *Rehabilitation Medicine: Principles and Practice*, ed. J. A. DeLisa, 2nd ed., 1,165–90). Philadelphia: J. B. Lippincott.

Brockman, R., P. Chamagne, and R. Tubiana. 1991. The upper extremity in musicians. In *The Hand,* ed. R. Tubiana, vol. 4, 873–86. Philadelphia: W. B. Saunders.

Dawson, W. J. 1992. The role of surgery in treating musicians' upper extremity problems. *Medical Problems of Performing Artists, 7,* 59–62.

Sataloff, R. T., A. G. Brandfonbrener, and R. J. Lederman, eds. 1998. *Textbook of Performing Arts Medicine,* 2nd ed. San Diego: Singular Publishing Group.

11

KEEPING YOUR
"EQUIPMENT" IN SHAPE

Musical instruments cannot make a sound by themselves; human physical participation must be an integral part of the music-making process. It follows naturally that the care and maintenance of the body—one's personal "equipment"—should be as important as that given to one's instrument.

We all see every day in print and on television, and hear on radio, a torrent of information about the advantages and suggested techniques of attaining and maintaining a healthy lifestyle. This concept has gained national attention and has undergone a great deal of expansion in the past two decades, fueled not only by the efforts of the media but also by the results of medical research. The public's increased awareness of, and interest in, all aspects of general health and wellness have resulted in a burgeoning personal involvement in the fitness and sports medicine boom of the last twenty years. However, the concept of wellness goes far beyond the basic goals of strength, endurance, and participation in sports and fitness; it properly emphasizes *all* aspects of health, including one's whole being and all life activities, and it embraces a number of diverse components.

LIFESTYLE DOs AND DON'Ts

With a few exceptions, the reader should not think of these lifestyle DOs and DON'Ts in terms of black or white but rather as a series of grays, each of which must be considered in the context of personal backgrounds, needs, and desires. Looking at these various components in this way also may help to make this chapter seem less like a lecture or sermon; my thoughts and suggestions are intended to be neither. My primary purpose is to present some concepts and ideas of health and prevention that may be useful to those instrumentalists attempting to both *attain* and *maintain* good health as a means of continuing their musical lives in an effective and enjoyable manner for as long as possible.

The mass of information on this subject presented by the various media can be confusing, especially to those who have not enjoyed the benefit of instruction or guidance in techniques needed to achieve health-oriented goals. Personal efforts in this regard may fall short for a variety of reasons, and the results obtained may be less than desired. On the other hand, excessive intensity of participation in normally healthy activities actually may be detrimental to some individuals. A typical example may be a "fitness fanatic" whose life revolves around physical conditioning activities and who needs a major daily fix of sports or athletic workouts to maintain a personal concept of health. In addition, the current national interest in, and emphasis on, dietary restrictions and supplements also can lead to improper eating behaviors, often to the detriment of one's body and lifestyle.

WHO CAN HELP

What is the best way to achieve the desired balance between the demands of active personal and professional lives and the degree of physical and mental health necessary to maintain one's interests and skills for the years to come? For most people, the first choice for guidance should be their family physician or general health counselor (internist, nurse practitioner, primary physician, or whatever title is appropriate). This person most likely possesses the necessary knowledge and information, and the patient should have no hesitancy or reluctance to discuss with him or her any concerns or requests for assistance.

Despite their professional training and experience, medical practitioners do not have all the answers for all people; some patients may have to consult other sources. In matters of musical performance, an instrumentalist should consult the music teacher or coach regarding concerns such as posture, body awareness, and other physical techniques that may help to prevent or minimize the effects of overuse activities during practice or performance. Families and friends also can be of great assistance, especially in the realm of interpersonal relationships and their effect on general well-being and performance abilities. Their nonmedical experiences frequently can be as helpful as those of a health professional to maintain one's ability to continue effective musical activities.

Aerobic workout and general fitness instructors, as well as personal coaches, also can be a valuable source of assistance. They generally possess the proper knowledge and many of the pertinent techniques for the maintenance of physical skills and generally are most willing to pass them along to their pupils. Learning more about such subjects as flexibility, strength, and endurance can prove useful to the instrumentalist who wants to preserve or prolong the physical, nonartistic aspects of performance during the ensuing years.

Making music is a physical activity; it requires a significant degree of muscular strength and endurance to maintain the fixed postures needed to facilitate effective breathing, as well as to perform the myriad fast, small hand movements for playing complicated and fluid musical passages. The need to maintain an optimum level of functional physical capacity is obvious; anyone who has experienced an injury or other physical difficulty that has limited or restricted this capability knows precisely what I mean. Maintaining and optimizing this capacity is mandatory to produce the best level of physical effort, not just for the immediate needs of musical performance but also for all life's activities in the years to come.

SOME DOs

Diet

One of the basic health philosophies relates to diet and body weight. Many sources tell us to maintain a satisfactory weight, and a multitude of diet and weight control regimens are available. Medical research continues to confirm the relationship between excessive body weight and the development of various illnesses, especially those involving the heart and blood vessels, diabetes, and (possibly) arthritis.

Neither science nor the media has yet solved the controversy surrounding the adverse effects of high blood cholesterol levels. Cholesterol is one of the normal components of fatty foods, which are a necessary part of all diets. In general, fats contain about twice the calories per gram (or ounce) of weight than do carbohydrates or proteins, and calories translate directly into pounds of weight. For those with a family history of high cholesterol or cardiovascular diseases, fats may play an even more important role and may need to be restricted. People who have a prominent family history of these types of diseases should consult a health professional regarding their specific situation and should obtain specific recommendations for maintaining cholesterol, lipoproteins (HDL and LDL), triglycerides, and other elements of body chemistry within a healthy range.

Here are some basic rules for weight control that most healthy people can follow, regardless of a particular metabolic or cardiovascular situation: eat at regular times each day, consuming three meals of adequate caloric size, and avoid snacks or between-meal foods. The best single method of maintaining or modifying one's weight is controlling portion size. Dividing the recommended daily caloric intake into three rather equal-sized meals serves to minimize the desire to snack between meals. Obviously, people with metabolic or nutritional problems should not follow this advice but instead consult their physician.

Exercise

As an element of health, exercise goes hand in hand with diet. A regular program of fitness and exercise can benefit most people in a variety of ways. First, it serves to restore or maintain the natural flexibility of joints and muscles, a condition that was taken for granted during childhood and that tends to be lost as the years go by. Increased tightness of all the body's musculoskeletal structures typically accompanies advancing age. This tightness often results in a greater susceptibility to muscle and tendon strains from normal or increased use. Muscles and ligaments are usually less resistant to injury when they become tight. In addition, using joints or muscle-tendon units at or near the extremes of their ranges often leads to overuse, strain, or inflammation.

Specific exercises and conditioning routines may help to improve or regain flexibility. The neck and back (spinal) muscles carry the greatest responsibility for maintaining a basic erect posture, but they also require a reasonable degree of flexibility to adapt to the demands of everyday activities. Some stiffness in all areas of the spine commonly develops gradually as a part of the aging process; however, a regular program of stretching and flexibility exercises can reverse or minimize many of these changes.

Another anatomic area subject to tightness is the forearm. The muscle groups located on both front and back surfaces of the forearm (the *flexors* and *extensors*) may become tight, sometimes simultaneously. A third region, one often overlooked, is the hand, which contains a number of small muscles in the spaces between the hand bones and at the bases of the thumb and little finger. These *intrinsic muscles* also can become stiff and tight from over-use, misuse, and disuse situations. This can result in localized hand pain and feelings of stiffness, tightness, and clumsiness.

Achieving and maintaining flexibility in tight structures involves both active muscle contractions and passive stretching actions. Because each joint requires different techniques, and since there are fewer written references on flexibility than on strengthening, I have included a list of appropriate stretching routines that can be useful to everyone with *normal* musculoskeletal systems. These exercises can be done conveniently in the rehearsal or warm-up room while fully dressed. They are designed for people with basically normal muscles and joints and with no medical conditions that would prohibit using these programs. I advise those musicians who have joint or muscle problems that could hamper their participation, or who have other pertinent medical questions or concerns, to consult their physician or other health professional for personal advice and guidance about strengthening, stretching, and other similar exercises.

All stretching exercise programs should be performed gently, slowly, and daily. Stretch each muscle group gradually to its maximum allowable length, and hold it there for a period of five to ten seconds; this should be accompanied only by a feeling of tightness—*not pain!* Perform five repetitions of stretch for each muscle group at each session, usually alternating with other groups so as not to injure or overuse any single one. Rest for several seconds between any two muscle stretches, so the tissues can "relax" and permit their blood supply to return to its maximum. For readers who are used to stretching their leg muscles prior to running or other physical conditioning activities, this program may seem very familiar; indeed it should, since all muscles, large or small, can benefit from the same basic type of exercise.

Finger joints

1. Stretch all fingers into extension, as far as they will go.
2. Move thumbs two directions:
   a. Backward into extension, in the same plane as the fingers and palm.
   b. Forward across the palm, trying to touch the pad of the thumb to that of the little fingertip.
3. Bend or flex the outer two joints of the fingers as far as they will go, trying to touch the fingernails to the outermost crease of the palm near the base of the fingers. After holding this maximum position for five seconds, slowly bend or flex the knuckles nearest the wrist, so that the fingers now form a fist. Then, squeeze the thumb over the clenched fingers.

Wrist joints and wrist, hand, and finger tendons

1. Place palms and fingers completely flat together, using only light pressure; hold the hands about six inches in front of the neck, with the fingers pointing straight up. While holding this position, slowly lift the elbows outward until the wrists are extended about 90 degrees (a right angle) or to their maximum.
2. Extend the elbow completely in front of you and make a gentle fist. Hold the fist, then bend or flex the wrist toward the palm as far as possible without opening the fingers out of the fist.

Elbows

1. [The previous exercise stretched or extended the elbow.]
2. Bend or flex the elbow slowly as far as possible and hold; most people should be able to touch the shoulder with the same hand at maximum flexion.
3. Extend the wrist and elbow simultaneously (as in pushing open a door). When the elbow is fully extended, rotate the forearm and hand 180 degrees, so the fingers point downward.

Shoulders.   These joints have the widest range of motion possible in any human joint. Try to move both upper extremities simultaneously, moving from the shoulder first, into all possible positions, and try to stretch the limb outward as far as possible during these movements. In addition, here are some specific stretches:

1. Bring the arms across the body, as in trying to hug one's self; reach around the body as far as possible.
2. Pull the elbows backward, as though trying to touch them behind the body.
3. Put hands behind the head; holding this position, bring elbows forward so they touch, then stretch them backward to their maximum.
4. Stretch the hands over the shoulders and reach far down the back.
5. Stretch the hands behind the back from below, trying to reach far up between the shoulder blades.

Neck
1. Bend forward to touch the chin to the chest; return to the starting position for a moment, then bend backward as though looking up to the sky.
2. While facing forward, tilt the head sideways (ear to shoulder) to the right; return to the starting position for a moment, and then tilt to the left.
3. While facing forward, rotate the head as far as possible to the right; return to the starting position for a moment, then rotate to the left.

Lower back (lumbar area)
1. While sitting, slowly rotate the torso to the right side, then to the left.
2. While sitting, bend the torso sideways to the right, then to the left. Keep the buttocks firmly on the seat.

3. While sitting with legs apart, bend the body forward so that the head moves between the knees.
4. Extend the lower spine backward into a maximum swayback posture while sitting on a stool or a backless chair.

As with any exercise or conditioning program, results will be gradual, and they depend on regular use of the program over long periods of time. Those who want to maintain flexibility and other aspects of conditioning can do at least some of these routines each day, incorporating them into a daily musical warm-up.

For those instrumentalists who possess more than the normal amount of laxity in their joints (a condition known as *hypermobility*), a somewhat different set of exercises is usually necessary. Such joints need a greater degree of motion control than their restraining ligaments can produce alone, so the surrounding muscles must come into play to limit these excessive motions. Adequate muscle strength is especially necessary in this group of people to safely control the hypermobile joints, and exercises designed to build muscle power can provide it.

Physical exercise has an additional positive effect on another group of people: those who have or are concerned about the development of *osteoporosis*. While a physician should direct the comprehensive treatment of osteoporosis, physical exercise has a positive, beneficial effect on everyone's bones. When muscles contract vigorously, they exert a pull on the bones to which they are attached and produce a positive stress within the bones. This in turn triggers a metabolic response to increase the production of bone substance, ultimately resulting in greater density and strength. This phenomenon is continuous throughout our lives and does not depend on age, gender, or degree of hormonal activity.

Regular Health Care

Maintaining a regular schedule of routine medical and dental care (preventive care) is another effective way for everyone, musicians and nonmusicians alike, to keep in shape. With the current emphasis on reducing health-care costs, regular checkups actually may save money in the long run. They also may facilitate the early detection of health problems (frequently making treatment easier and less complex) and thus may avoid or minimize some of the complications of disease or treatment. More and more health insurance plans now pay for "wellness" care, including regular checkups, immunizations, and other preventive measures.

Medications

Another important principle of health maintenance is to use all medications properly, whether prescribed by a health professional for a specific condition or obtained over the counter. Self-diagnosis and self-medication can be fraught with dangers, including the likelihood of making the wrong diagnosis or choosing the wrong medication. It can also delay obtaining the correct type of care.

As people age, they usually develop a variety of medical conditions or problems and may see a number of different physicians. Each may prescribe different medications for a specific condition. Using many different drugs at the same time may lead to problems caused by incompatibilities and troublesome interactions among the various medications. Each person must do their utmost to prevent such incidents by informing every health professional of all current and past medical problems, of the name and dosage of each medication currently being used, and of the name of each prescribing physician.

How We Can Deal with Aging

Everyone must accept the fact that physical and mental changes occur with the passage of time, and another important DO is to deal effectively with aging. No one can deny the passage of time, nor the bodily changes that accompany it; the Peter Pan approach simply is not realistic in promoting and maintaining good health. On the other hand, it is not wise merely to accept or give in to the effects of aging without making some personal effort to minimize their negative aspects.

One of the most difficult situations in any instrumentalist's life (professional or otherwise) is knowing how and when to make changes when the stability or effectiveness of one's musical life is threatened by the problems of aging. A wide variety of possibilities for change do exist, and the musician should evaluate each one critically, based on personal musical experiences, the current playing demands, and physical capabilities. It is possible to make many different modifications in such areas as repertoire, performance focus, intensity of involvement, instrument played, and the types of groups with whom one plays. For an occasional performer these changes may not solve such problems; however, only after all prior treatment and rehabilitation efforts have failed should one ever consider discontinuing musical performance.

SOME DON'Ts

Every individual must make decisions about these DON'Ts based on his or her own personal experiences, philosophy, education, and musical requirements. It is incumbent upon everyone to learn as much as possible about these negative practices and how they can affect the human body and its functions.

Tobacco

Smoking and the instrumentalist—it should be obvious to everyone that the respiratory effects of tobacco smoke are uniformly destructive, both from the standpoint of decreased endurance resulting from chronic bronchitis and from the real danger of cancers affecting the lungs, mouth, and larynx. Even nonsmokers are at risk because studies show that exposure to second-hand smoke can produce lung cancer. This fact places even the nonsmoking instrumentalist or singer who performs in a smoke-laden club atmosphere at risk.

A second disease linked directly with the use of smoking tobacco is *emphysema*, also known as *chronic obstructive pulmonary disease*. In this disease, some of the small air sacs in the lungs enlarge to many times their normal size and thus cannot empty as efficiently when we exhale. This condition is not malignant, but it can affect all musicians, not just woodwind and brass instrumentalists. The shortness of breath and rapid, labored breathing that accompany emphysema negatively affect a person's endurance for all physical activities. Unfortunately, even nonsmokers may develop this condition, and all known forms of treatment are designed to control, but not cure, the problem.

Even without the presence of these diseases, woodwind and brass instrumentalists cannot be at the top of their performance capabilities when they are smokers. Smoking decreases one's capacity for rapid, forceful breathing—the ability to move large volumes of air quickly—so necessary for many instruments. Smoke also irritates the airway—throat, windpipe or trachea, and bronchial tubes or bronchi—and leads to troublesome, untimely coughing.

Alcohol and Drugs

We now know that alcohol and other recreational drugs have the potential for producing a number of deleterious and dangerous effects on the body, especially when abused, yet so far we haven't seen reports of a significant decrease in recreational drug use. While the decision to use such drugs is strictly personal, users recognize and accept the consequences of such actions.

Improper Body Use

Knowingly using one's body for any activity in an abusive manner or trying to exceed its capabilities for a particular task constitutes improper body use. Excessive or improper physical use of the human body certainly is not illegal or otherwise restricted, but it, too, may produce sprains and strains of the joints, muscles, and tendons, often accompanied by pain and decreased function. They may occur during one's musical life as well as at other times, such as on the job or in recreational pursuits. Heavy lifting and participation in some extreme sports are two examples of activities that can place a person at increased risk of physical injury. These abusive or overuse practices, most of which can be minimized or prevented, can limit physical abilities and the endurance for musical performance as well as for many other functions in life.

Respiratory Diseases

Of the communicable diseases, the ones most important to instrumentalists involve the respiratory system. The common cold, bronchitis, and even pneumonia are easily transmitted and received by casual and indirect contact, and all of these can limit musical performance capabilities. Maintaining good physical condition may help to avoid contracting these illnesses or to deal more effectively with their symptoms. Preventive vaccines are frequently of little benefit, since each one is generally designed to protect against only a single type of virus or disease. That said, I still advise musicians to discuss the pros and cons of flu shots with their health professional. On the other hand, avoiding close contact with anyone who is sneezing, coughing, or showing other evidence of respiratory disease and washing hands thoroughly with soap are always good advice.

Noise

Noise is an unavoidable part of everyday life. Under certain circumstances, excessive noise levels can produce serious and permanent damage to the hearing apparatus. The condition of *noise-induced hearing loss* has been causally linked to the prolonged or repetitive exposure to loud sounds, whether produced by music, machinery, airplane engines, gunfire, or any other source. This type of hearing loss is not confined to the mature musician but can develop in younger individuals who are exposed regularly to high noise levels (whether as a spectator at a rock concert or as a performer who has spent many years sitting in front of brass musicians or percussionists). In addition, high noise levels may occur as part of nonmusical occupations.

PREVENTION

In this section I present a number of strategies that may be helpful to the instrumental musician in relation to many of the subjects I've discussed in this book. Not every method of prevention is applicable to any one person, but most can avail themselves of several of these methods at various times during their musical lives.

Good Body Mechanics

The music-making environment should be of primary importance, and since so much time is spent there, it deserves a most careful evaluation. One of the musician's first tasks in this regard should be to look critically at the physical conditions that surround and affect practice and performance, and determine what steps might be taken to optimize them. Second, the performer's body must operate in an efficient, comfortable fashion while playing and be able to adapt to many variables in the environment; this is necessary to maximize individual abilities and minimize the chances of overuse difficulties or injury. Achieving both these goals requires, among other things, employing some special physical techniques usually referred to as *good body mechanics*.

The foundation for playing most instruments is correct seating, using chairs that fit the person properly and are designed for long periods of comfortable sitting. An appropriate chair should have its seat perfectly level or slope slightly toward the front and placed high enough for the musician's legs and feet to rest comfortably on the floor. This allows the low back to assume its most comfortable and stable posture without being subjected to strain. A seat cushion with a triangular cross-section, thicker in the back than in the front, may allow a player to sit comfortably in a chair whose seat position would normally force him or her into a backward-leaning posture. Other types of chair modifications are available to deal with special physical requirements and individual anatomical variations; several chair manufacturers have produced models that address some of these special needs.

Using various supports, including such items as a neck strap for the clarinet, oboe, or English horn or a floor peg for the latter, may minimize the strain of supporting a heavy instrument. Bassoonists and bass clarinetists also may benefit from the use of a floor peg, similar to that employed for the cello or contrabassoon (figure 11.1). Both these devices usually may be obtained from instrument repair or accessory shops. If a bassoon strap causes excessive pressure on the performer's neck, looping it over the left or right shoulder instead may relieve the problem (figure 11.2). This modification does not alter the support or balance of the instrument and has the added advantage of allowing unrestricted use of the chest and diaphragm muscles for proper breathing and efficient sound production.

Many woodwind and brass performers are doublers and often must travel with several large and heavy instruments, stands, and so forth. The physical acts of transporting and setting up these instruments can produce injuries such as strains of various muscles and joints (just ask any percussionist about this). Using good body

Figure 11.1.   **A bass clarinet fitted with a floor peg for support**

Figure 11.2.   Note the neck strap being worn over the bassoonist's left shoulder to decrease neck strain.

mechanics, including proper lifting and carrying techniques, is essential in preventing such difficulties. Performers may obtain information regarding these techniques from a physical therapist, orthopedic surgeon, or rehabilitation specialist, as well as from many primary physicians. In general, when lifting off the floor, the knees should be bent, the back straight, and elbows extended so that the legs provide the force of lifting. When lifting something from table height, the body should be close to the load, elbows flexed, and knees bent if needed.

Over the past decades, people have advocated a number of physical disciplines and philosophies of bodily movement as a way

to assist musicians and dancers in achieving and maintaining efficient posture and body awareness. These can be used in both therapeutic and preventive ways and have gained increasing accept-
ance among a variety of performers. Two of these methods are
those of Alexander and of Feldenkrais (see chapter 9); specially
trained practitioners teach and promote their techniques worldwide. Learning and using one of these movement disciplines can
be an effective aid to practice and performance for many instrumentalists and should be considered as another option to help
achieve and maintain good body mechanics and awareness.

Hearing

The increasingly common condition of noise-induced hearing
loss (NIHL) can be prevented or minimized by the use of sound
attenuators. These are small devices that decrease the sound level
by 9, 15, or 25 decibels. The attenuator is fitted into an earplug or
mold, which is placed inside the instrumentalist's ear canal (figure
11.3). Newer models are self-contained, avoiding the expense of

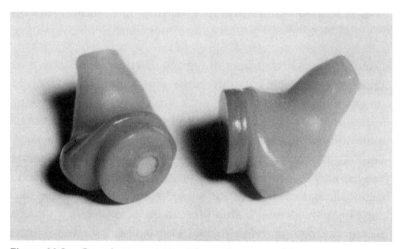

Figure 11.3.   Sound attenuators with custom ear molds

having custom molds made. A 15-decibel (Db) attenuator can decrease noise levels by as much as 75 percent, helping to minimize further ear damage and hearing loss.

One comparatively minor disadvantage of this device is that it produces some alteration in the performer's perception of sound quality and intensity. Using these attenuators emphasizes the loudness of the wearer's own instrument (because the sound is then conducted more efficiently through the bones of the skull than through the air) and at the same time decreases the sound levels of other instruments (whose sounds reach the ear by air conduction). However, most people can learn to adapt to this with practice and in the long run may benefit through the preservation of their hearing acuity.

Dental Health

A musician may not consider the importance of dental health and its associated preventive strategies until problems arise. The facial structures are as crucial to the production of music as are the fingers, and any alterations that result from aging, illness, or injury may have a serious effect on the wind player's embouchure and sound production. Regular dental examinations often may disclose early changes of disease or degeneration. Appropriate treatment of these problems in their early stages is generally more effective, less time-consuming and expensive, and requires less musical adaptation by the player.

Restoration of the myriad complex dental and facial structures after injury or illness depends on the health professional's knowledge of their prior conditions and anatomy; a set of dental models can be of tremendous help in this regard. These plaster models of the upper and lower teeth and jaws (figure 11.4), preferably made early in the performer's adult life, can be used later as a guide for reconstructing or revising tooth and jaw alignment and shape to prior playing contours but not to the so-called "ideal" or "normal"

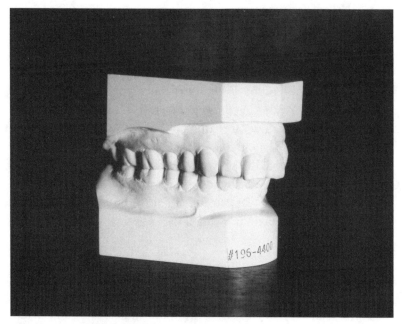

Figure 11.4.   Dental models

condition. The performer takes these models along from one city to another as occupational change may require; thus they can be readily available to a dental professional if the need arises. String players, such as violinists and violists who depend heavily on the chin and jaw while playing, also may benefit by obtaining a set of dental models.

General Health

Early, proper care of all health problems is one of the mainstays of a healthy life; it can help prevent or minimize troublesome conditions such as complications from injury or illness, incomplete or fragmented care for many medical difficulties, and prolonged disability that can interfere with rehabilitation and return to performance. Everyone should strive to seek proper evaluation and care for *all* problems, both related and unrelated to music making, and not depend on themselves, their family, or friends to take that responsibility. The timely and skilled assistance of health professionals can save a career in some instances.

Increasing numbers of performers now are able to receive the benefits of specialized knowledge and skilled care provided by performing arts medicine specialists, both physicians and therapists. Although this medical specialty has been recognized for less than twenty-five years, it has expanded to include practitioners throughout the United States and other parts of North America, Europe, and the Pacific.

SOME FINAL THOUGHTS

In concluding this chapter, I offer for consideration a few statements that reflect my personal philosophy, both as a musician and a physician:

- Our musical art and talents are gifts that we have nurtured and cultivated in many ways for many years; for most of us, our music *is* our life.
- We all must do what we can to preserve this talent and to increase our skills for as long as we wish; no one else can do this for us.
- Therefore, it is incumbent upon each of us to learn as much as possible about our bodies and their functions—those factors so necessary to our art and its expression.
- The more we know about, and can provide preventive care for, ourselves, the longer and more successfully we can use our natural talents, advancing our art and providing enjoyment for all who listen to our music.

NOTE

Portions of this chapter were adapted from articles by Dr. William Dawson that appeared in *The Double Reed*, Winter 1994 and Winter 1998; © The International Double Reed Society, Idaho Falls, ID. Reprinted by permission.

SUGGESTIONS FOR FURTHER READING

Bondurant, N. 1992. Movement, music, and the Alexander technique. *The Double Reed, 15(1),* 59–61.

Howard, J. A., and A. T. Lovrovich. 1989. Wind instruments: Their interplay with orofacial structures. *Medical Problems of Performing Artists, 4,* 59–72.

Kennicott, P. 1994. The best seats in the house? *Symphony, 45(2),* 28–31.

Mackenzie, C. 1991. C. McKenzie comments on a performing arts medicine lecture [Letter to the editor]. *The Double Reed, 14(2),* 59.

Zimmers, P. L., and J. P. Gobetti. 1994. Head and neck lesions commonly found in musicians. *Journal of the American Dental Association, 125,* 1,487–96.

WEB RESOURCES

Alexander Technique: www.alexandertechnique.com

Embouchures.com, Inc.: www.embouchures.com

Embouchures.com, Inc., provides information based on the book *Broken Embouchures* by Lucinda Lewis, the principal horn of the New Jersey Symphony Orchestra and a faculty member of the 2005 annual symposium of the Performing Arts Medical Association.

Feldenkrais Method: www.feldenkrais.com

Health Promotion in Schools of Music (HPSM): www.unt.edu/hpsm/

HPSM addressed the health risks associated with learning and performing music. Information on the findings is on their website.

International Forum on Adaptive Musical Instruments for Persons with Disabilities: onehandwinds.unk.edu/forum/index.php

The forum welcomes posts on both congenital and acquired disabilities.

Medical Problems of Performing Artists (MPPA): www.sciandmed.com/mppa/

MPPA is the official journal of the Performing Arts Medicine Association. Abstracts of current and past issues are available online.

National Association for Music Education (MENC): www.menc.org

The MENC position statement on health in music education (www.menc.org/connect/surveys/position/health.html) details health concerns as well as guidelines for music teachers.

National Association of Schools of Music (NASM): www.nasm
.arts-accredit.org
NASM has added a recommendation to its accreditation guidelines for
member schools to provide students with health information that pro-
motes awareness and prevention of performance injuries. The study
"An Overview of Health Issues for Performing and Visual Arts Students" is available for purchase. Click on "Publications" then on "As-
sessment and Policy Studies."

Performing Arts Medicine Association (PAMA): www.artsmed.org
PAMA is an organization of physicians and other allied professionals
dedicated to improving the health care and treatment of performing
artists through education, research, and teaching. A more extensive
bibliography on musicians' medical problems can be found on the site,
as well as links to health-related sites.

University of Nebraska (Kearney) One-Handed Woodwinds Program:
www.onehandwinds.unk.edu/

GLOSSARY OF TERMS

Acupressure. A derivative of acupuncture, using manual pressure on specific body points instead of inserting needles.

Acupuncture. An Eastern practice of inserting needles into specific points on the body for the purpose of "channeling" energy flow and treating various conditions.

Agonist/antagonist. Muscles or groups of muscles whose contractions produce opposite movements of a body segment.

Alexander technique. A philosophy and method of body awareness and alignment, designed to prevent and treat some problems of performers.

Analgesic. Pain-relieving.

Arthritis. Any inflammation of a joint.

Atrophy. Loss of substance; wasting (as in muscle).

Bone scan. A diagnostic test using small amounts of radioactive isotope, which is taken up by the bones and is measured or scanned to determine the amount of blood flow to the bones.

Carpal tunnel syndrome. A group of symptoms caused by pressure on the median nerve at the palm (front) side of the wrist; these include pain, numbness, tingling, and/or weakness in the hand and several fingers.

Cartilage. The resilient, smooth, glistening substance found on the ends of most extremity bones, forming a gliding surface at a joint.

Cataract. Clouding of the lens of the eye, usually resulting in decreased visual acuity.

CAT scan. Computer-assisted tomography, or a diagnostic X-ray test in which the tissues are imaged in thin "slices"; computer-assisted techniques allow three-dimensional evaluation of bones and some soft tissues.

Chronic. Long-lasting or persistent (as opposed to *acute*).

Co-contractions. The simultaneous contraction of agonist and antagonist muscles about a given joint.

Connective tissues. A group of bodily structures including ligaments, muscles, tendons, capsule, and fascia; these hold various portions of the body together or help move the skeleton.

Crepitus. A sensation of irregular motion felt around inflamed tendons or a collection of air under the skin; it can be described as bubbly, rubbing, crackling, or clicking.

Cubital tunnel syndrome. A group of symptoms caused by pressure on the ulnar nerve at the elbow; these can include numbness, tingling in several fingers, and muscle weakness or clumsiness in the forearm or hand.

Decompression (of nerves). A surgical procedure in which external pressure on a nerve is relieved by various methods.

Deformity. An abnormal appearance, shape, or position of a body part.

Degenerative joint disease. One form of arthritis, usually seen in an older population and related to the effects of physical "wear and tear"; also known as *osteoarthritis* or *degenerative joint disease*.

Disc, herniated. An abnormal bulge or protrusion of one of the cushioning structures that are located between the vertebrae or spinal bones.

Dupuytren's contracture. A condition characterized by thickening of the flat connective tissues of the palm and fingers, producing nodules (lumps) and/or tight cords that limit spreading or extension of the fingers.

EMG. Electromyogram: a diagnostic test that measures the electrical activity of muscles; it indirectly measures the function of the nerves that supply those muscles.

Extensor. Relating to stretching out of a joint; this term also may include the muscles that perform this motion or refer to the surface of the limb where they are located.

Fascia. Flat bands of connective tissue that separate layers or compartments of muscles, blood vessels, and/or nerves.

Feldenkrais. A philosophy and technique of body awareness, similar to but relying more on exercises than the Alexander technique.

Flexor. Relating to the bending or "closing" of a joint; this term also may include the muscles that perform this motion or refer to the surface of the limb where they are located.

Fracture. Any break in a bone.

Glaucoma. A condition characterized by increased pressure of the clear fluid in the front of the eyeball.

Herniated disc. *See* Disc, herniated.

Homeopathy. A healing philosophy that employs very dilute substances for the treatment of disease processes that are often caused by large amounts of the same substances.

Humerus. The arm bone, located between the shoulder and the elbow.

Hyperextension. The condition or act of extending a joint excessively or beyond its usual range.

Hypermobility. The condition of being able to hyperextend one's joints.

Inflammation. A series of complex physical and chemical responses of tissues to various unpleasant stimuli, such as overuse, infection, injury, or surgery. These may include local redness, heat, swelling, pain, and decreased function.

Internist. A specialist (MD or DO) in internal medicine or the nonsurgical problems or conditions of patients.

Intrinsic muscle. Small muscles that are located entirely within the hand or foot; contrast with extrinsic muscles, whose fleshy or contracting portion lies outside the hand or foot and which is attached by a tendon to it.

Joint. The space where two bones contact each other and where movement may occur. The joint is contained within a fibrous sac or capsule.

Laceration. A cut or open flesh wound with clean, sharp edges.

Ligament. A fibrous structure connecting two bones and forming part of a joint; it limits the motion of these bones relative to one another.

Metacarpal. One of the five bones in each hand (not the wrist or finger bones).

MRI. Magnetic resonance imaging: A diagnostic procedure employing magnetic and radio waves that cause the bones and soft tissue structures to produce a series of shadows or images; these images assist in the three-dimensional evaluation of many physical conditions. No radiation or X-rays are involved in this test.

Muscle. An organ that can contract or shorten its length by complex chemical processes.

NCV. Nerve conduction velocity: A diagnostic nerve test that measures the speed of conduction of an electrochemical nerve impulse and gives information about the function of the nerve itself.

Nerve, median. A nerve, extending from the shoulder to the hand, that supplies sensation and motor function to many parts of the upper extremity, especially the thumb, index finger, and long fingers.

Nerve, motor. A nerve that goes to muscles, supplying them with impulses to produce contraction.

Nerve, peripheral. Any nerve that extends outside the spinal cord to the body, arms, or legs.

Nerve, sensory. A nerve that carries sensation-describing impulses from a peripheral area of the body to the brain and/or spinal cord.

Nerve, ulnar. A nerve in the upper extremity that supplies sensation and motor function to many areas, especially the ring and little fingers.

Neurologist. A medical specialist (MD or DO) who deals with the nonsurgical treatment of diseases and conditions of the nervous system. Contrast with *neurosurgeon*, who treats many of these same problems surgically.

Neurophysiologist. A medical scientist (usually MD) specializing in the functions of the nervous system and who often performs evaluations, monitoring, or testing of these functions.

Nurse practitioner. A nurse (RN) with specialized training in evaluating and treating various medical problems, including taking patient histories and performing physical examinations; these activities are done under the supervision of a physician (MD, DO, or others).

Osteoarthritis. A type of arthritis seen usually in an older population and characterized by degeneration of the joint cartilage and secondary thickening of the adjacent bone.

Osteoporosis. A condition of bones characterized by decreased density and increased susceptibility to fracture; it is common in older people, especially women, and also can be caused by disuse of the affected area.

Overuse syndrome. A collection of musculoskeletal symptoms (a *syndrome*) characterized by pain and decreased function affecting a specific anatomic area. It is produced by excessive physical use (force, duration, and/or repetition) of that area while performing a specific activity, musical or otherwise. Other terms used for this condition include *cumulative trauma disorder, repetitive strain injury, occupational strain syndrome, repetitive motion disorder, occupational cervicobrachial disorder, tendinitis,* and *regional pain syndrome.*

Performing arts medicine. A medical specialty concerned with the evaluation, treatment, rehabilitation, and prevention of conditions and problems affecting performing artists (such as musicians, dancers, and actors).

Performing Arts Medicine Association. The national association of medical and paramedical practitioners who are involved with performing arts medicine in the United States.

Physiatrist. A medical specialist who deals with the nonsurgical evaluation, treatment, and rehabilitation of various musculoskeletal medical conditions.

Physician. A person specially trained in diagnosing, treating, and otherwise caring for people with medical problems and conditions. These individuals have completed graduate training programs and have qualified for a variety of doctoral degrees, including those for *allopathic physicians* (MD), *osteopathic physicians* (DO), *chiropractic physicians* (DC), and *naprapathic physicians* (DN).

Placebo (effect). Lessening or relief of subjective symptoms after treatment with a "medication" that contains no active disease-treating ingredients.

Podiatrist. A specialist (doctor of podiatric medicine, or DPM) who evaluates and treats problems and conditions of the foot and toes; both medical and surgical treatments may be employed.

Presbyopia. A condition produced by aging of the eyes and characterized by decreased ability to focus on near objects.

Pronate/pronation. The movement of turning the hand or foot into a palm-(or foot-)down posture; the position thus achieved by such an action.

Psychiatrist. A medical physician (MD or DO) specializing in the diagnosis and treatment of mental problems and diseases.

Reflexology. A treatment philosophy based on the premise that massage of certain points on the body stimulates a flow of energy to various bodily organs for the purpose of assessing and improving their function.

Rehabilitation. The process of restoring a patient to maximum possible anatomic and functional levels after a disease, condition, or injury.

Rheumatoid arthritis. A type of arthritis or joint disease characterized by inflammation of the tissues around the joint itself and caused by unknown mechanisms that seem to involve the immune system of the body.

Rheumatologist. A medical specialist (MD or DO) who evaluates and treats in a nonsurgical way the various arthritic and connective tissue disorders and conditions.

Shiatsu. A healing practice similar to acupressure, except that the specific body points are massaged.

Spasm. A condition of extreme, and usually painful, localized muscle contraction; it is not normal and often is seen as a protective mechanism for other injured structures.

Spur. An abnormal bony prominence, usually adjacent to a joint and often related to osteoarthritis or previous injury.

Steroid. A series of chemical compounds, some of which are produced by our bodies, some in the laboratory. They have many different effects on the body, including relief of inflammation, building of muscle tissue, and both male and female hormonal functions.

Surgeon, hand. A surgical specialist (usually an MD) who is involved with all problems relating to functions of the hand and wrist; this individual may have specialty training as an orthopedic, plastic, or general surgeon.

Surgeon, orthopedic. A surgical specialist (MD or DO) who is involved with the diagnosis, treatment, rehabilitation, and prevention of diseases, conditions, and injuries relating to the musculoskeletal system.

Syndrome. A group of symptoms relating to, or produced by, a specific medical condition.

Synovitis. An inflammation of synovial tissue, which lines the cavities of joints and surrounds tendons; it facilitates gliding of tissues on one another.

Tendinitis. An inflammation of a tendon in any area of the body.

Tendinitis, degenerative. Tendinitis produced or related to under-lying degeneration, or "wear and tear" changes, in the tendon.

Tendon. A firm, fibrous, flat or rope-like structure that attaches the fleshy or contracting portion of a muscle to a bone and causes the bone to move when the fleshy portion contracts.

Tenosynovitis. An inflammation of the coverings or gliding tissues about a tendon.

Therapist. A health-care specialist who is involved with the physi-cal and/or functional treatment of patients with varying types of problems, often under the direction of a physician. Several types of therapist exist, including physical, occupational, hand, mas-sage, speech, music, art, and recreational.

Thoracic outlet syndrome. A group of symptoms caused by com-pression of nerves and/or blood vessels in the neck, usually be-tween the upper ribs and the muscles at the side of the neck.

Trauma. Injury of any kind.

Trigger digit. A form of tenosynovitis characterized by local thick-ening in a finger tendon that causes a clicking or catching sen-sation when the tendon moves.

Vitalism. A supernatural theory of an energy that is believed re-sponsible for all the activities of a living organism; also known as "vital force" and by many other synonyms.

INDEX

ABOUT THE AUTHOR

Dr. William J. Dawson was a musician long before he became a physician, but he has successfully balanced both careers. Following medical school at the University of Illinois in Chicago, he became a certified specialist in orthopedic surgery and was in private practice for nearly thirty years. He is associate professor emeritus of orthopedic surgery at the Feinberg School of Medicine, Northwestern University, and after retirement he switched his focus to performing arts medicine. Dr. Dawson is immediate past president of the Performing Arts Medicine Association. He has written more than 120 scientific articles, books, and textbook chapters dealing primarily with hand and upper extremity problems of musicians and serves on the editorial board of *Medical Problems of Performing Artists*. He has presented numerous lectures, seminars, and clinics on performing arts medicine topics in the United States, Europe, Australia, and Asia.

Musically, Dr. Dawson has been an active performer for more than fifty years as a member of numerous bands, orchestras, chamber groups, and choirs in the Chicago area. Although his major instrument is the bassoon, he plays instruments from all musical groups and especially enjoys those with very low ranges. Dr. Dawson currently is the principal bassoonist and contrabassoonist of the Northwest Symphony Orchestra and the Community Orchestra of the Music Institute of Chicago, as well as a regular member of the Glenview Concert Band. He maintains a high school bassoon studio in Northbrook, Illinois, and also teaches privately at other north suburban high schools.

Membership Invitation

MENC: The National Association for Music Education
invites you enjoy the benefits of membership in
the only professional association dedicated to music for all!

Are you a music teacher?
A music education student?
A parent? A caregiver? Retired? Collegiate? Corporate?
Or simply a friend of music?

There's a place for everyone in music education.

MENC: The Largest Arts Education Association on Earth.

Come see where you belong: www.menc.org

1-800-828-0229 (outside the U.S., call 703-860-4000)

Music. Learn it. Live it. Love it. For Life.*